Teaching Social Competencies
in Post-Conflict Societies

Susanne Krogull, Annette Scheunpflug
and François Rwambonera

Teaching Social Competencies in Post-Conflict Societies

A Contribution to Peace in Society and
Quality in Learner-Centred Education

Waxmann 2014
Münster • New York

This book is based on the authors' experiences with projects run by the
Council of Protestant Churches in Rwanda and financed by
Bread for the World – Protestant Development Service Germany

Bibliographic information published by die Deutsche Nationalbibliothek
Die Deutsche Nationalbibliothek lists this publication in the
Deutsche Nationalbibliografie; detailed bibliographic data
are available in the internet at http://dnb.d-nb.de.

Print-ISBN 978-3-8309-3081-5
E-Book-ISBN 978-3-8309-8081-0

© Waxmann Verlag GmbH, 2014
Steinfurter Straße 555, 48159 Münster, Germany

www.waxmann.com
info@waxmann.com

Cover Design: Inna Ponomareva, Münster
Cover Picture: © Athanase Rutayisire
Setting: Sven Solterbeck, Münster
Print: SDK Systemdruck Köln GmbH & Co. KG, Köln

Printed on age-resistant paper, acid-free as per ISO 9706

Printed in Germany

All rights reserved. No part of this publication may be reproduced, stored in
a retrieval system or transmitted in any form or by any means, electronic,
electrostatic, magnetic tape, mechanical, photocopying, recording or
otherwise without permission in writing from the copyright holder.

Contents

Foreword by the Council of Churches of Rwanda. 7

Foreword by Bread for the World/
Protestant Development Service Germany 11

Introduction 13

1	**Social Competencies, Learner-Centred Education and Peace** 17	
1.1	The Need for Refocusing Education towards Peace 17	
1.2	Understanding Social Competencies. 25	
1.3	Knowledge and Skills Required for Social Competencies. 31	
1.4	Social Competencies and Peace in Society 38	
1.5	Social Competencies, Learner-Centred Education and Educational Quality 43	
1.6	Conclusion: Social Competencies and Self-Efficacy as Learner-Centred Educational Responses in a Post-Conflict Society 50	
2	**Teaching Social Competencies** 53	
2.1	Content: Through Students' Eyes 53	
2.2	Methods: Cognitive Activation. 60	
2.3	Classroom Management: Empowerment and Recognition 68	
2.4	Linking these Elements in Program 76	
3	**Implementing Social Competencies in Schools** 78	
3.1	Teacher Training 78	
3.2	Involving the Stakeholders 91	
3.3	Follow-up and Supervision 94	
3.4	The Trainers. 98	
3.5	Quality Management 100	
3.6	Financial and Funding Requirements 102	

4	**Does it Work? Results from Research** 106
4.1	Empiric Analysis of Learner-Centered Education 106
4.2	Findings 1: Improvement of Activation in Class 116
4.3	Findings 2: Encouragement of Students' Personal Development 118
4.4	Findings 3: Enhancement of Competences for Democracy and Peace 118

Epilogue – Cooperation in a Global Context 121

References 124

About the Authors 137

Foreword by the Council of Churches of Rwanda

As part of its strategic plan for quality of education, the Council of Churches of Rwanda (CPR) successfully pioneered the Learner-Centred Education (known as Participatory Active Pedagogy or PAP in Rwanda) as a teaching methodology in the Rwandan education systems. The notion of quality education dates back to CPR's inception in 1963. A key area set up by the founding fathers was education for the Protestant children who had been discriminated against during Belgian colonial rule. When the 23 churches and church-related organisations membership of CPR defined their vision of education, they emphasised that schools should not only be channels for the acquiring general knowledge and self-reliance, but also venues for strengthening social, human and Christian values.

Learner-centred education was inaugurated in Rwanda during the years following the 1994 genocide against the Tutsi. The worst tragedy in the country's history completely destroyed its social fabric, and disrupted political, economic and cultural institutions. Political will and determination were fundamental to any reorganization of Rwandan society. However, decrees alone cannot mend the social fabric. A country derives from social, human, spiritual and cultural values. During the difficult post-genocide era, the new Rwandan government's call for national unity and reconciliation challenged civil society – and the churches in particular – to offer their perspectives on the most crucial areas, such as education. Hence the National Office for Protestant Education of the CPR put forward the concept of an innovative and engaging educational system. Fortunately, the Protestant Development Service Germany/Bread for the World, one of the historical partners of Rwandan churches, was extremely interested in the idea and offered their full support.

The objectives of learner-centred education consist of strengthening the teachers' pedagogic capacities, upgrading managerial capacities of school principals and administrators, as well as those responsible for the educational components in churches and church-related organisations. By pursuing this process systematically over time, BNEP hoped to refocus the mind-set of all the Protestant schools by changing the behaviour of the teachers, staff and heads of schools. Likewise, students needed a new approach to the learning process so they could begin to acquire human, social, Christian and democratic values. It's clear that instituting learner-centred education was the right approach and has been instrumental in healing the deeply wounded Rwandan society.

The context of the pre- and post-genocide crisis was made of trauma, suspicion, fear, mourning, the absence of concentration in classrooms, and a total disorientation of everyone. With learner-centred education we tremendously contributed to the revitalisation of social cohesion, the promotion of good, transparent and democratic governance in the schools. We are sure that this will impact on society. In June 2011 an annual prize for the best school performance in a national contest ranked over 2,000 secondary schools nationwide. Assessment results clearly indicated that the top performing Protestant schools were those that had adopted the learner-centred methodology.

In the 1970s the world-acclaimed Brazilian educator and ecumenist, Paulo Freire, launched his famous attack against what he called the "banking education" by proposing a "liberation pedagogy." This revolutionary concept challenged our efforts towards a learner-centred educational approach. In the new world of "liberation pedagogy", learners no longer took as gospel the supposedly all-knowing teacher's pronouncements. Now the teachers expand their students' vision by interacting and dialogue with their students to increase their awareness of themselves and their relationship to the outside world.

Paule Freire's concept expanded on the work of his pedagogic forefathers including Alfred Binet, Johann Heinrich Pestalozzi and others. Unfortunately, Paulo Freire never had disciples in Rwanda before the genocide. Our antiquated school system taught students to memorise concepts instead of thinking critically. This produced generations of graduates who adhered individually and collectively to sectarian, hatred and genocide ideology. Lacking a sense of self-worth, Rwandans could be so easily abused and manipulated by ill-intentioned persons and ideologies. Without fundamental changes, our society could easily have died.

The genesis of the book you hold in your hands is rooted in an evaluation undertaken in 2010/11 headed by Professor Doctor Annette Scheunpflug in cooperation with our team from the Department of Education of the CPR. The findings of the evaluation were shared among various stakeholders in the education field including: the Minister of Education and his collaborators, local and international participants UNICEF, USAID, the Catholic Office of Education, various universities and many others.

Readers of this book must decide for themselves whether CPR achieved its initial aim to change the mind-set of our Rwandan education system. The many insights gleaned during the field research and subsequent presentations of findings had been a motivation to produce this book. Both Prof. Dr. Annette Scheunpflug and her colleague Mrs Susanne Krogull as well as Mr. François

Rwambonera (director of the National Office of Education in CPR) and his collaborators were keen to present their discoveries from their respective academic and practitioner perspectives. On behalf of the Protestant Council of Rwanda, I sincerely thank the research team; I express my gratitude to Brot für die Welt/Protestant Development Service Germany for their continued support of CPR. I convey my deep gratitude to the CPR's partners in education in Rwanda, particularly the Ministry of Education for its frank collaboration with churches in promoting quality education in Rwanda. To all teachers and students, please accept our gratitude. Happy reading!

Kigali, June 2013

Dr. Tharcisse Gatwa

Foreword by Bread for the World/Protestant Development Service Germany

It is an honour and a pleasure to present this important piece of work on school education in a post-traumatic society. This book represents 15 years of cooperation between EED / Bread for the World – Protestant Development Service[1] and the Protestant Rwandan education sector. It provides a theoretical framework for designing teacher trainings in post-traumatic circumstances, using concrete examples from our partner organizations. It also discusses the long-term impact of new concepts in education to the students' lives and to society.

In 1997 the National Bureau of Protestant Education within the Protestant Council of Rwanda initiated teacher-training reforms with support from the Protestant Development Service. The challenges in post-genocide Rwanda were huge: schools lacked even basic infrastructure and facilities; worst of all most former teachers had fled during the conflict. The country seemed populated by deeply traumatized individuals. Several questions arose: How to continue after such a humanitarian disaster? Could the children of the genocide perpetrators even attempt a new beginning along with the children of the victims? How could schools in general contribute to reconciliation and peaceful development? Could Protestant schools and Protestant pedagogy in particular make a difference?

Believing that indeed education could make an important difference to the country's rehabilitation, the National Bureau asked for our support in terms of teacher training. Based on positive experiences in Cameroon, the National Bureau developed its own education concepts and methodology aimed at building peace and reconciliation. All the elements – procedures towards active personality development no matter how disadvantaged the student or teacher, proactive involvement of women, participatory methods for problem solving and conflict resolution during school lessons – were consciously based on Protestant values.

In 2011 – after 12 years of innovative teacher training – a scientific impact evaluation was carried out. It revealed remarkable insights such as students

---

1   Evangelischer Entwicklungsdienst (Protestant Church Development Service) has merged with Brot für die Welt (Bread for the World) in October 2012. Its name is now Brot für die Welt – Evangelischer Entwicklungsdienst (Bread for the World – Protestant Development Service) Germany.

in schools, where learner-centred education was introduced, feel less afraid, understand the lesson structure better and participate more in class. Teacher violence has markedly decreased and students have greater self-esteem. Teachers focus less on competition in class and use more student-centred learning activities. Teachers deal more constructively with conflicts. Thus we can conclude that learner-centred education leads to higher democratic competencies for peace.

My appreciation goes to the main participants of the teacher training program and scientific evaluation. I am grateful for the enormous efforts they undertook and for their successful work despite the difficult times. I hope that by publishing this book we will not only enrich discussions on pedagogy for peace but will also contribute to increased support for education in fragile environments.

Berlin, June 2013

Prof. Dr. Claudia Warning

Director International and Domestic Programmes
Bread for the World – Protestant Development Service

Introduction

This book addresses the challenges of designing school education in post-traumatic societies. When life slowly gets back to normal after war, lessons need to be designed in a way that students and teachers can get back at least a little of normality and that the lessons themselves contribute building a peaceful society. This book presents school experiences from post-genocide Rwanda reflecting them against the international discourse on peace education. This implies giving an overview of the different approaches to peace education. This book would like to encourage educational stakeholders to consistently orient school education towards promoting and encouraging students as well as implementing democratic cooperation and learner-centred education.

When life starts getting back to normal in a society which has been at war, schools have to cope with enormous development tasks:

- The social climate is often still oriented on mistrust and suspicion, which cannot easily be broken by school.
- Often – as is the case in many places in Rwanda – schools are visited by relatives of victims and offenders likewise, leading to existential feelings and sorrows influencing school.
- It is often is not possible within a society to talk about what has happened and to come to terms with it discursively, reason for which may be political or because of the force of the events or a combination of both.
- Communication about what has happened is often engrossed by a state-enacted interpretation of history, making it impossible to openly account for and address.
- Teacher and students need to process their own traumatic experiences and are under a great deal of inner pressure.
- The demands on school education made by society regarding the facilitation of coherence are tremendous.

This book presents one way of dealing with these challenges in class. It is about developing, implementing and realizing micro-didactic elements of democracy in class by opening the lessons to participatory and active pedagogy. We understand this pattern of classroom-management as a contribution to peace education. Through such education, the teachers' and students' self-esteem as well as self-consciousness are strengthened. Therewith they are potentially supported in addressing the development challenges in fragile societies towards peace and democracy.

This book is based on experiences from Rwanda, where the program was developed after the genocide and has since then also been implemented in the Democratic Republic of Congo. It has been developed by the team of the National Bureau of Protestant Education (Bureau national de l'Enseignement Protestant, BNEP) of the Protestant Council of Rwanda in Kigali, supported by Dr. Christian Grêt, a Swiss educator. From 1997 to 2012, they've been concerned with implementing participatory and active learning. Since 2000, 2,500 teachers have been trained and more than 830.000 students have benefitted from the program.[1] The program is called "Participatory and Active Pedagogy" (Pédagogie active et participative, PAP) and has been financially supported by the German Protestant Development Cooperation (Brot für die Welt/ Evangelischer Entwicklungsdienst, EED).

Learner-Centred Education:
The Program of Participatory and Active Pedagogy

The post-genocide situation in Rwanda brought about a number of challenges to be faced by education. In September 1994 the order to re-open the schools was given. But the situation was severe: Many qualified teachers had been killed, while others had taken refuge in neighbouring countries. The material damage was clearly visible; the school infrastructure was destroyed or dilapidated. In addition, the social and psychological problems were without precedent. Schools functioned with multiple problems only, some visible (as economic, physical, and material challenges), but the biggest ones often hidden, silent or suppressed (psychological, moral, and psychosomatic problems). It is obvious that teachers, as well as students, were affected and marked by these problems. There was an extreme need to use teaching methods which would ease the acuity of these problems.

In these challenging times, the National Bureau of Protestant Teaching of the Council of Protestant Churches of Rwanda decided to explore the possibilities of developing and implementing such pedagogy. With help from a Swiss educator and financial support from the Protestant Development Cooperation

---

1   The calculation is based on the World Bank's teacher-student-ratio.

Germany the team developed a teacher training program in participatory and active pedagogy in 1997. Implementation started in 1998.

Between 2000 and 2012 a total of 2,500 teachers in more than 350 schools were trained (32% of all protestant nursery schools, 37% of all protestant primary schools, and 27% of all protestant secondary schools), reaching more than 830.000 students.

This book is divided into four chapters. Chapter 1 explains the relationship between teaching social competencies and peace education, referring specifically to the situation in post-conflict states. Chapter 2 describes the educational concepts and the changes it implies for the classroom. Chapter 3 addresses the question of how to organize capacity building for teachers and teacher-trainings. Finally, chapter 4 presents findings from the study on learner-centred education, and evaluates whether such a program actually works. This book is translated to Kinyarwanda and available in a Rwandese edition.

The following people have contributed to the book: Pierre Claver Bisanze, Rudolf Heinrichs-Drinhaus, Immaculée Mukantabana, Samuel Mutabazi, Jean-Baptiste Ndamukunda, Monique Nyirandikumana, Athanase Rutayisire, and Zacharie Zikama, and a lot of teachers from the schools through texts, testimonials, and thoughts and discussions, especially Innocent Gasana, Violette Mukayisenga, Anastasie Mukaruberwa, Marlène Mukandoli, Anathalie Munganyinka Félicité Musabyemariya, Théophile Mutuyeyezu, Jean Bosco Ndimubanzi, Jean Baptiste Ndigendereho, Silas Nsengiyumva, Capitolina Nyirabazamanza, Josée Nyiramana, Agnès Nyirangirimana, Athalie Nyiranzigiyimana, Athanase Rutayisire, Gérard Ugirashebuja, and Césarie Uwabaganwa.

The evaluation of the program was supervised by a consultative council. We thank its members for their especially constructive and helpful comments: Dr Tharcisse Gatwa (chairperson), Mgr Augustin Mvunabandi, Mgr Alphonse Rutaganda, Rev. Dr Elisée Musemakweli, Dr Erasme Rwanamiza, Dr Faustin Habineza, Dr Joyce Musabe, Narcisse Musabeyezu, and Fortunée Kubwimana.

This book grew out of research supported by grants from the Protestant Development Cooperation/Evangelischer Entwicklungsdienst (EED), Deutsche Gesellschaft für Internationale Zusammenarbeit (GIZ) Germany; Stiftung Bildungspakt Bayern, Bavarian Federal Ministry for Education, and Sparda-Bank Oberbayern, Germany. We express our thanks for this support and confidence in our work. The training team is based in the very supportive climate of the office of the Council of Protestant Churches in Kigali, Rwanda. The research team thanks their inspiring colleagues and efficient and supportive administration at the Friedrich-Alexander University Erlangen-Nuremberg and

Otto-Friedrich-University Bamberg, Germany. We are very grateful to Emmanuel Nkurunziza and Marie Claire Niyoyita for their intensive and professional work in translating our questionnaires into Kinyarwanda. Initially called upon to proofread the English text, Jennifer Gampell ended up rewriting most of it and worked long and hard to create a book written in English. We express our deep thanks to her.

Nuremberg/Kigali, August 2013

Susanne Krogull
Annette Scheunpflug
François Rwambonera

1 Social Competencies, Learner-Centred Education and Peace

This chapter is about the link between peace education and social learning in schools. It explains the relations between education, conflicts and peace. The specific concept of the peace education training focused in this book is explained as focusing on social competencies and self-esteem. The meaning of social learning and how to understand the psychological mechanisms related to it are described. The contributions of social learning to peace and social cohesion as well as to learner-centred education and quality in education are addressed. Theoretical assertions are illustrated with experiences from a Rwandan project in learner-centred education, called "Participatory and Active Pedagogy (PAP)".

1.1 The Need for Refocusing Education towards Peace

Education in Post-Conflict Situation

Many studies have dealt with the impacts of conflict on education (cf. UNESCO 2010). Conflicts such as war and civil wars negatively impact education on many levels: the proportion of the population with formal education, the average years of education attained, the literacy rate, death or displacement of teachers, staff, and students. In post-conflict situations, a country often faces lack of educational infrastructure (destroyed buildings, lack of educational material, few or no experienced teaching professionals, etc.). In addition, the country must confront physically or mentally traumatized students, parents, and teachers and the society at large. Conflicts often result in decreased access to school and increased teacher absenteeism. In most post-conflict countries, enrolment declines (cf. Lai & Thyne 2007, on Germany Akbulut-Yuksel 2009, on Germany and Austria Winter-Ebmer 1998, on Cambodia Merrouche 2006). The quality of education also suffers due to shortages in basic necessities such as food, water and school materials. The academic year may be interrupted or shortened due to conflict (Shemyakina 2006, 15). Conflicts also exacerbate existing marginalization in societies. Due to the economic difficulties brought about by war, those in the poorest strata of society may take their children out of school and put them to work in order to maintain their existing consumption levels (Shemyakina 2006, 15).

1 Social Competencies, Learner-Centred Education and Peace

Post-conflict reconstruction in education poses immense challenges. Governments must operate in environments marked by high levels of instability and uncertainty and low levels of capacity. Rebuilding a broken school system in the face of chronic funding deficits and teacher shortages poses particularly acute problems (cf. UNESCO 2011, 20). Children and teachers are on the front lines of conflict. They face physical attacks, rape and other sexual violence, as well as recruitment into armed forces and abduction. School infrastructure is often attacked (cf. UNESCO 2011, 142–146). Mass displacement is also a real barrier to education.

> **The post-conflict situation in Rwanda**
>
> More than two-thirds of teachers in primary and secondary schools were killed or displaced during the Rwandan genocide in 1994 (Buckland 2005, xi). Teachers were targets of the attacks and educated adults were more likely to die in the conflict (de Walque & Verwimp 2009). Yet Rwanda is hailed as a post-conflict educational success story, since enrolment levels had returned to their pre-conflict levels by 1999, five years after the genocide (Buckland 2005; Lopez & Wodon 2005b). Those who were school-aged children during the genocide are still impacted by their experiences. Akresh and de Walque (2008) showed that genocide-affected children completed half a year or 18% less education than unaffected children. Work by Lopez and Wodon (2005a; b) confirms these findings. The genocide affected progression through the educational system, rather than overall participation in school (Akresh & de Walque 2008). It also negatively impacted the educational attainment of some regions more than others (Akresh & de Walque 2008).
>
> Conflict causes a decline in enrolment. The educational attainment of the richest cohorts was most negatively affected, while that of the poorest cohorts remained at its relatively low pre-conflict levels. One explanation is that war tends to affect secondary enrollent more than primary enrolment (cf. Shemyakina 2006). Secondary education requires more specialized resources than primary and is harder to establish and maintain during or after armed conflict. Additionally, students of secondary school age quit to enter work or military service, especially during times of economic uncertainty. The educated classes of Rwandan society were actively targeted during the conflict, which also contributed to the decrease in the average years of education for cohorts during this period.

When large numbers of young people are denied access to decent quality basic education, the resulting poverty, unemployment and sense of hopelessness can be powerful recruiting tools for the armed militia. In rural areas, unemployed,

1 Social Competencies, Learner-Centred Education and Peace

undereducated young Rwandan men figured prominently among the perpetrators of the 1994 genocide (cf. UNESCO 2011, 16 f.). Disarmament, demobilization and reintegration facilitated a return to education for former Rwandan combatants; many took up vocational training opportunities (cf. UNESCO 2011, 20 f.)

Education is not only affected by conflicts, but often does play a crucial role in fostering conflicts and contributing to conflicts (cf. Davies 2004; Davies et al. 2011). Unequal access to education may be a source of marginalizing people and creating social distrust and frustration. Education may manipulate and reinforce fragility by manipulating structures, curricula and textbooks and by this harming and violating parts of the population. Observing the ambivalent influences of education on the genesis and dynamics of violent conflicts can help demystify its apparent peace-building power. The negative influences of educational structures and processes on conflict in society are obvious. The destructive potential of education doesn't only exist when education is abused for the purpose of propagating war propaganda or when teachers incite one ethnic group against another. Schools can become a place of abuse or corporal violence, and thus cultivate a culture of punishment as revenge (cf. for Europe and the USA Harber 2004; 2009; CIE 2006; Leach & Michell 2006; for the current German debate Bergmann 2011; for Africa Davies 2010; Hunt 2007; Kruss 2001). Even though corporal punishment is legally banned in most school systems on the African continent, it remains a part of daily school life. The formal education system often exacerbates societal conflicts, especially when it (re)produces socio-economic disparities and causes social marginalization or compartmentalization. The system also teaches concepts of identity and citizenship that deny a society's cultural plurality and lead to an intolerance toward "the other." Education is a key medium for mobilizing ethnicity in service of escalating conflicts. Corruption in schools does destabilize societies. Schools can advocate violence by allowing and thus tacitly promoting repressive or structural violence. This occurs by naming, shaming, or bullying students, creating taboos, prohibiting conversation, or excluding particular groups from education such as certain ethnic or religious minorities, girls and young women. High fees and compulsory school uniforms often exclude the poorer segments of the population (cf. Davies 2004; 2010; Salmi 2006). Schools unwittingly promote violence as a normal element of daily life if the root causes of violence are not openly discussed during class or if teachers ignore these issues due to fear of political repercussions (cf. for Asia Davies et al. 2009; for Europe Donelly 2004). Schools can be a place of sexual abuse and violence.

Schoolbooks can harden gender stereotypes and discriminate against individuals. Kent's study of a South African township school demonstrated how concepts of masculinity and femininity are constructed during class and how this can contribute to gender inequality (cf. Kent 2004). Leach & Dunne described their research conducted in 12 schools in Botswana and Ghana wherein "boys actively constructed a masculinity in which they marked out their physical and verbal space to distinguish themselves from, and claim superiority over, girls" (Leach & Dunne 2007, 199). In their study on girls' school attendance in northern Uganda, Murphy et al. (2011) showed that a number of factors hampered school attendance, attending school, including financial constraints and cultural barriers. This study also showed that "girls faced self-doubt and a lack of self-efficacy about their ability to achieve in schools, which was compound by bullying from peers and stigma from the community." (Murphy et al. 2011, 167) Girls who survived sexual violence experienced were particularly prone to these feelings (cf. for Malawi Bisika et al. 2009).

Education may contribute to conflicts when educating people to blind obedience and non-reflecting ideologies, not allowing speaking up. In Rwanda until today, education is mainly organized in the class-room in a chorus speaking way, not allowing individual learning, personality or individual meanings. To change this habit of schools is a crucial and difficult task in post-conflict-education which is often neglected. (Cf. concerning current education tasks and issues relating to the fields of conflict Retamal & Aedo-Richmond 1998; Arnold et al. 1998; Tawil & Harley 2004; Seitz 2004; Lenhart 2010.)

These different factors clarify under which conditions education can help exacerbate violent conflict. However they may also be used positively: under the perspective of the greatest possible avoidance of destructive elements and the minimization of risks, positive criteria for the constructive conflict sensitivity of education systems may be stated. A key question in the relationship between education and conflict concerns how education systems deal with diversity in society with regard to access to education and curriculum, both institutionally and conceptually. Developing a conflict-sensitive educational system requires a holistic approach that takes into account the potentially constructive and destructive impact of education in all its guises. Transforming education systems in post-war societies can only be successful after a comprehensive critical analysis of the destructive potential of the previous education system, including curricula and common educational practices. The common assumption, "whatever is done to ensure more education, contributes to promoting democratic attitudes" (Schell-Faucon 2001, 56) has been vehemently

1 Social Competencies, Learner-Centred Education and Peace

contradicted by recent analyses in the context of ethnic conflicts (cf. Bush & Saltarelli 2000; Smith & Vaux 2003): "Simply providing education does not ensure peace" (Smith & Vaux 2003, 10).

This double bind of education toward peace in being at the same time a source of peace but a root of violence as well gives a special responsibility to education. In his work "Education After Auschwitz" (1966), the philosopher Theodor W. Adorno described the demands placed on schools as follows: "The premier demand upon all education is that Auschwitz not happen again. Its priority before any other requirement is such that I believe I need not and should not justify it. I cannot understand why it has been given so little concern until now. To justify it would be monstrous in the face of the monstrosity that took place. [...] Every debate about the ideals of education is trivial and inconsequential compared to this single ideal: never again Auschwitz." (Adorno 1966, 92)

Peace education or peace building education?

In the international discourse on peace education, Bush and Saltarelli (2000) distinguish between "peace education" and "peace building education". "Peace education" is understood as a top-down approach, often instituted by an organization or government. It can have positive effects as well as negative ones, such as manipulating history for political purposes or using education as a weapon in cultural repression. Peace education tends to use a "rather narrow recipe-book approach" (23), relying on workshop trainings where the skills and techniques taught are necessary for dealing with specific conflict situations. "Peace building education – like peace building itself – would be a bottom-up process driven by war-torn communities themselves, on their experiences and capacities. It would be firmly rooted in immediate realities, not in abstract ideas or theories. It would be applied, immediate, and relevant, which means that it cannot be restricted to the classroom." (Bush & Saltarello 2000, 23) "Peace building education" takes a holistic view of education: "formal, informal and non-formal; content and teaching methods; arts and sciences; child-centred and adult-centred" (23). Thus it addresses not only the manifestations of violence but also its causes.

In this book we follow the tradition of understanding peace education in the broader and normative understanding of peace-building education as outlined by Susan Fountain: "Peace Education [...] refers to the process of promoting the knowledge, skills, attitudes and values needed to bring about behaviour changes that will enable children, youth and adults to prevent conflict and violence, both overt and structural; to resolve conflict peacefully; and to create the conditions conducive to peace, whether at an intrapersonal, interpersonal, intergroup, national or international level" (Fountain 1999, 1).

Overwhelmed in the classroom

Schools therefore play a critical role, not just in equipping children with knowledge and skills, but also in transmitting values and creating their sense of identity. These tasks become more complicated in post-conflict regions or states wherein classroom instruction poses manifold problems:

- Children of victims often sit side by side with children of offenders. How should they deal with such tragic family histories? Children allege mutual delinquencies in the absence of any social mechanisms to adequately verify them. Suspicion, insecurity and solitude characterize the climate in class.
- Many students have lived through horrific events. Their trauma and grief integrate into the learning process and hamper it. Students become suddenly fearful or burst into tears; they experience deep frustration and crises of trust. These experiences need to be acknowledged and addressed in class. In this context, a classroom and school climate characterized by low concentration in class, high absenteeism, and low readiness to learn often develops.
- Many teachers are completely overwhelmed by their situation. On one hand, they and their families have lived through the same horrible experiences and suffered the same traumas as their students. That they have neither the necessary qualifications nor the support to adequately cope with the situation is also profoundly overwhelming.
- Additionally, refugees and internally displaced people often enter classrooms and influence and/or disrupt the learning environment. Some speak different languages, have different cultural backgrounds and come from countries with a different culture of learning.

Concepts of peace and post-conflict education

To implement much-needed reconciliation into school life in a conscientious manner, the following different but complimentary objectives and concepts are discussed in the field (cf. on conceptual questions for an overview Harries & Morrison 2003; Haußmann et al. 2006; Schröder et al. 2008; Bajaj 2008; in historical-conceptual perspective Nipkow 2007):

- *Concepts of commemoration and naming conflicts*: Schools may contribute to the reconciliation process by instituting a culture of commemoration, naming conflicts and educating pupils on conflict history from different perspectives. This mode of education works best in societies where the past conflict is dealt with in society as a whole. For example, after World War II "Anti-Holocaust-Education" was specifically implemented in Germany by the Americans. Students in classrooms nation-wide were shown films about the Nazi atrocities and thus had to acknowledge it. This style of education clearly labels offenders and victims and distinct moral positions can be taken. The historical genesis of the conflict as well as the conflict itself is addressed.

- *Concepts of affirmative peace education:* Schools can contribute to peace and social cohesion by providing insights on why violence and exclusion are unappealing options. The resolute condemnation of violence and forcible and offensive integration of race, ethnic and gender issues becomes an important component of the learning process. This mode of education encourages non-violent communication, changing perspectives and using inclusive language. Events of the past receive a new perspective and new social relations can be established.
- *Concepts of fostering peace and democracy in the classroom:* By teaching and applying democratic practices in the classroom and in daily school life, education contributes to training democratic forms of conflict resolution. Avoiding corporal punishment and practicing participatory forms of decision-making in class elicits democratic forms of cooperation. These acquired competencies later find use in society and democratic comportment.
- *Concepts of strengthening the individual by self-esteem and self-efficacy:* Once students are taught how to become responsible individuals, authoritarian attitudes and demagogy lose their fascination. Education should focus on expanding participation and strengthening young persons' self-esteem and self-efficacy. Such a student-centred approach creates a greater sense of personal sovereignty and emphasizes non-violent social interactions. In this model, students and their needs become the focus of attention.

The positive pedagogy approach of learner-centred education or Participatory and Active Pedagogy underpinning this book considers the last two of the above four strategies. It is the *first long-time and evaluated educational program which consequently aims to enhance self-esteem in post-conflict-education*. Changing perspectives, using inclusive language, raising self-esteem and self-efficacy, instilling democratic cooperation in class, is focused. Lessons are no more organized in a chorus-speaking manner but with group- and partner-work, students investigating by themselves. Henceforth this concept is referred to as "strengthening of social competencies" of learner-centred education or, as Rwandan colleagues have called their program, "Participatory and Active Pedagogy" (PAP). This kind of peace pedagogy emphasizes the role of the educator as one who helps students develop a more positive and elaborate concept of their own.

François Rwambonera – former head, National Bureau of Protestant Education: Why I started PAP

The social context after the genocide was totally new. It was practically impossible to return to the dynamic pedagogic innovation that existed before the events of 1994. At the same time, it was obvious that life at school could not continue as before, ignoring completely what had happened and how the genocide had affected social, mental, emotional, and psychological reference points. The entire national social context, particularly at the school level, had changed completely. There was a dire need to use teaching methods to ease the severe problems encountered. The new pedagogy was needed to facilitate working on many different dimensions of a person simultaneously, especially as concerns students and teachers. This pedagogy should foster learning, support reconciliation and social harmony, reconstitute security and internal peace, recreate trust and self-esteem.

During 1995, I held several reunions with the principals of schools from different regions to exchange ideas about the difficulties encountered in their schools. They identified many problems on the professional, social and psychological level. Both teachers and students faced a severe and complex situation. Some of the problems identified included:

- Introversive disturbances: trauma, mourning, crisis of trust, despair, frustration, absence of internal peace, despair, sudden fear;
- problems of social cooperation: suspicion, revolt, rejection, hate, aggressiveness, insecurity, solitude;
- problems relating to school: finding school disgusting, low concentration, refusal of authority, lack of communication skills.

Our team was faced with the task of finding a teaching methodology to help to deal with these problems and challenges. Classroom methods no longer corresponded to the context in which people were living and continue to live. We needed to promote more active and participatory methods and these were put into practice within the classroom: A pedagogy, where the child plays an active role, takes initiative, expresses him- or herself, looks for solutions to situations of presented or experienced problems; a pedagogy where the teacher ceases to be a "distributer of knowledge" but rather plays the role of an animator and organizer of the students' groups. In short: a learner-centred pedagogy.

PAP in the (post-)conflict Democratic Republic of Congo

Since 2001, the Community of Baptists in Central Africa (CBCA) has been offering training in learner-centred education/PAP in the North- and South-Kivu provinces of Eastern Congo. The training programme establishes a democratic methodology in schools in order to abandon corporal punishment from schools and enable students to "take their destinies into their own hands and commit themselves to a peaceful society" (EED 2011, 11).

The training supports teachers in recognizing the needs of students and organizing lessons in a more democratic manner without fear or corporal punishment. Methods that enable students to access and acquire knowledge are emphasized. PAP gives priority to autonomous working and collaborative learning (see Paccolat 2012).

1.2 Understanding Social Competencies

What is the learning concept behind peace education through participatory and active pedagogy? Why does activation in class lead to more social competencies? The terms social learning, PAP, and social competencies are highly valued, yet their conceptual underpinnings are often poorly defined.

Taking a very general approach, Hannah Arendt described social competencies as competencies which enable people "in der Welt zusammenzuleben", ["to live together in the world"] (Arendt 1958). Welsh & Biermann present a quite simple and all-encompassing definition: "Social competency refers to the social, emotional, and cognitive skills and behaviors that children need for successful social adaptation" (Welsh & Biermann 2001). Argyle (1972) defines social competencies as "the knowledge and application of an appropriate behavior in interactions in social situations" (Argyle 1972). But what is meant by "successful social adaptation;" and what constitutes "appropriate behaviour in interactions?" It is often defined as a person's competency to act as a full member of a given society (Runde 2001) as well as the ability to constructively balance the tension between asserting one's own interests and adapting to the interests of others. "Social competencies reflect adjustment in the family, school, work, in society at large, and in old age, requiring more context specific definitions of the construct, as well as a focus on particular facets of social competency, such as empathy, self-control, trust, respect for other people, or civic engagement" (Schoon 2009, 4).

> **François Rwambonera: Motivation for PAP**
>
> We wished for a pedagogy offering conditions favourable for learning; where students are at the centre of the learning process; which values a person's intellectual, affective, social, and universal potentials (Gordon 1981; Maria Montessori by Benoît Dubuc 2005).
>
> Looking at the socio-political context after the genocide, we wanted pedagogy to help the students develop logical reasoning, objective argumentation and a spirit of critical analysis. This educational vision brought a new element to our educational system where previously classroom education depended on a teacher who knew everything and distributed his or her knowledge to the students. Often, students were reduced to listening, writing what they were told, and rote learning their notes (Muhimpundu 2002; Grêt 2009).
>
> We wanted the teacher to help students learn by focusing on their success. The students should be empowered to assume responsibility for their learning process, become active participants in class, and perform research individually or as a group. This concept is new in our education system, particularly when students need to present their findings in front of the class and the teacher. We realized that this approach created an entirely new attitude among primary school students – a spirit of creativity and organization. This approach not only makes it easier for students to participate, but also helps develop a sense of autonomy in the learning process. (Piaget by Marie-Françoise Legendre 2005)
>
> Group work, a key element in class as well as in our teacher training, has become an effective tool to facilitate learning and creating social harmony in class. Students take up different roles within their groups. They learn to cooperate and listen to each other, to understand the complementarity of ideas and take democratic decisions. They develop a positive sense of belonging to the group. Thus due to the practice of PAP, the pedagogy of memorizing which once occupied a prominent place in our education system has diminished in favour of a pedagogy of activity and group work.

Social competencies refer to individuals, but are also situation-dependent

Social competencies refer to individuals and must be assessed in reference to them. Yet they also relate to social interactions because the tension between an individual's relationship to him/herself and others manifests in social situations. Whereas reading competency is relatively independent from the situations in which people read, social competency varies according to the situation.

1 Social Competencies, Learner-Centred Education and Peace

Social environments mark an important dimension for social behaviour and the acquisition of social competencies.

Social competencies are value related

Dictators who manipulate a population or crime bosses who successfully manage their gangs could be seen to demonstrate a version of social competency. Yet while dictators and criminals do find the balance between asserting their own interests and adapting to the interests of others, manipulation exists outside the rubric of social learning. In our understanding of the term, social competencies are committed to public welfare and represent humane democratic values.

Social competencies reflect changing global situations

Social competencies reflect different cultural standards because they are value-based and situation-dependent. Social interactions vary from country to country, often requiring different social competencies. As the world moves increasingly toward globalization, societal values and situations can change (cf. Schoon 2009, 2). Social competencies in many societies have referred primarily to authority and cultural group patterns. In a world dominated by individualism and individual performance, those social competencies are now undergoing deep changes.

Social competencies reflect individuality

Often social competencies are misunderstood as submitting to peer-pressure, as when people are excluded from social groups because their particular view supposedly disturbs a certain order. Alternatively, social competencies can be misunderstood as submitting to the rules of a particular group. Looking at social cohesion in society, social competencies e.g. in schools can be misunderstood only as conformity. But social competencies are particularly necessary when dealing with divergent perspectives and negotiating different positions. Social learning is therefore, among other things, closely related to the pedagogy of conflicts. Thus, socially competent behaviour is explicitly understood as the "behavior which contributes to realizing one's own objectives while at the same time looking for social acceptance" (Kanning 2003, 15).

Example: Transformation of social competencies due to societal changes

The psychologists Chen and French (2008) proved that the country's dramatic economic growth affects highly recognized social competencies in China. For example, both parents and their children are becoming less submissive to authority. In contrast, social competencies such as assertiveness, autonomy, and individuality are gaining in importance. Similar changes are also occurring worldwide. In a globalized world society, competencies such as self-regulation, self-confidence and autonomy are on the rise.

François Rwambonera: Teaching students in mourning

This describes the situation of one student, though I encountered numerous similar cases when I visited primary schools after they reopened in 1994.

One day in February 1996, I visited a 5th grade math class in a primary school in the North. The teacher gave explanations and afterwards the students were given individual exercises to do. Some did them; others seemed distracted or were dreaming. One 11–1/2 year-old student did something completely different. He scratched a mixture of drawings and phrases on his paper. The teacher, circulating the class, approached him. She started bawling him out, but the boy merely lifted his head, looked her in the eye, got up and left the room.

I got up and taking the paper he'd left at his desk, I followed him. I found him leaning against the classroom wall. There he stood immobile, hands in his pockets, one leg bent, foot and head against the wall. His open eyes and implacable gaze gave the impression that he was staring at something far away. Torrents of tears ran down his face and fell on his shirt. In front of this picture I felt impotent; emotions rose up inside me as if I too wanted to cry. I tried to contain myself and with great difficulty succeeded in suppressing my emotions. The image of the boy still remains in my spirit.

Eventually I greeted him in our Kinyarwanda language, extending my hand toward him. Instead of answering he nodded his head and gave me his hand. Without letting go of his hand, I invited him to talk to me for a moment, which he accepted. We went to a secluded place and sat down on large stones. We chatted a little and after about fifteen minutes he told me about his family situation. He was an orphan and lived with his paternal grandmother.

He said he wasn't in the mood for studying anymore; he couldn't concentrate on what the teacher asked him to do; he couldn't bear the teacher's remarks, indeed they annoyed him. We had a good time together, but it was very moving. Our conversation probably lasted around 40 to 50 minutes, after which we went back into class. I came to understand that this boy was mourning his parents whom he had lost, and that he hadn't received any sympathy from his teacher.

Before leaving, I talked to the teacher about this special case. She recounted that before the war and the genocide against the Tutsis, this boy was very strong and did well in class. After these sad events he became lazy, ill-disciplined and aggressive towards the other kids.

I invited her to adopt a more positive approach toward the boy, to show him more sympathy in order to help him with his life as an orphan.

I realized that in order to teach better, this teacher needed other pedagogical tools to better understand the new post-war and post-genocide context. It affirmed my conviction of the extreme necessity to change the teaching methods and adopt new ones to effectively help sooth these kinds of problems among the teachers and the students.

Self-concept as a base of social competencies

Social competencies therefore are based on the ability to know about the self – or the so called self-concept. Students' overall concepts of themselves consist of different subsets, which Shavelson et al. (1976) term social, emotional, physical and school self-concepts. Together these determine the general self-concept (cf. fig. 1), also known as "self-esteem".

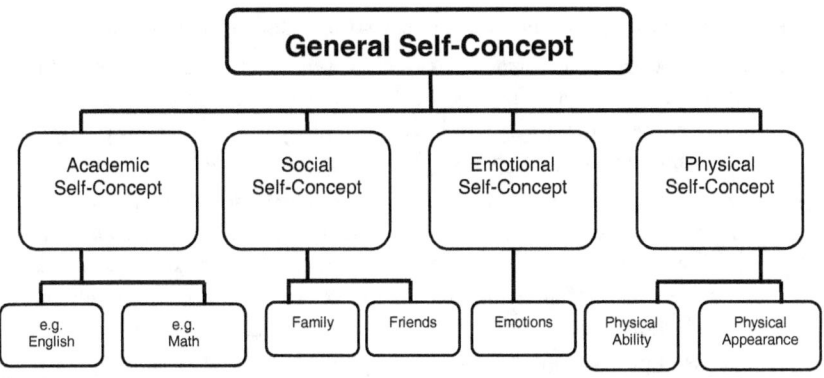

Fig. 1: Structure of self-concept, largely based on Shavelson et al. 1976

The academic self-concept includes the cognitive convictions of a student regarding scholastic capabilities in specific domains (cf. Moschner 2001). A student's experiences at school affect the academic self-concept yet al.so impact the social, emotional and physical self-concepts. These in turn influence the student's overall self-concept, or self-esteem. Students in class want to be recognized for the totality of their personality. When only academic achievement is valued, the other three aspects of a student's self-concept are often forgotten. Thus low academic achievement can easily – and unintentionally – negatively influence other domains of a student's self-esteem. Conversely, a good academic self-concept positively affects the other components of self-esteem. Students who feel academically competent deal with tasks more efficiently, are less prone to anxiety or depression and go on to become successful in their professional lives (cf. Moschner 2001; Shavelson 1976; Hannover 2012). Moreover, the degree of this "self-efficacy" is a good predictor for academic performance.

Experiences from Rwanda: PAP and self-esteem

The PAP program aims to systematically strengthen feelings of self-esteem and self-efficacy among teachers and students in order to contribute to social coherence and peace. Teachers must learn to become more aware of their students' social needs and build their self-esteem and self-confidence by giving them more freedom. By creating a social climate that promotes better learning and social opportunities for the students, the PAP program reinforces the teacher's role as facilitator and organizer in their learning process.

Violette Mukayisenga, teacher at a nursery school: Raising self-esteem

When I started working at nursery school, I believed that some students couldn't change their bad character and always held the parents accountable for the situation. After the formation in PAP in 2007, I quickly realized that everything was possible and I had a role to play in changing a student's outlook.

One year, four year-old boy Moïse joined my 2nd grade nursery school class. He spent the first two months of class without saying a word; he barely even moved. When his mother came to school she explained that Moïse had experienced heart problems since the age of three months. I integrated the kid into play groups and asked him questions, but Moïse never answered. Later, I gave him some responsibilities, like standing in front of the class and calling out the names of those who did well in a game. At first, he only pointed with his finger without speaking, but little by little he started talking in class and his parents were happily surprised by his changes. Today, Moïse is the first to tell stories to the others; he even makes up stories just because he likes to talk.

Extra-curricular activities such as school-theatre, music, sports, community-engagement etc. can also enhance a student's self-esteem.

Anastasie Mukaruberwa, secondary school teacher:
Extra-curricular activities

Before PAP was introduced in our school in 2007, the majority of the students were shy and afraid to speak in public. But after our formation in PAP, I took the initiative to start different extra-curricular activities for the students such as a debating club, theatre group, cultural dance group, etc. The various groups participated in competitions with other schools and won lots of prizes. The theatre group was so successful, it was even asked to perform in front of school authorities and teachers.

When I asked the students about the secret of their success, they stated it was thanks to the teachers and the new teaching methods. The extra-curricular activities also helped build trust between teachers and students because we all worked together towards common objectives. We became partners. This changed relationship also influences life in the classroom. Thanks to PAP, the students' academic achievement also improved.

1.3 Knowledge and Skills Required for Social Competencies

Skills leading to social competencies

To enhance social competencies and self-concept, what have to be trained? Social competencies require a multitude of attitudes, values, skills, knowledge structures and forms of communication and behaviour. No simple relations exists, nor can any uniformly applicable definition be found in the academic literature (cf. Erpenbeck & v. Rosenstiel 2003; Reißig 2007). Various groups of researchers posit many different factors (cf. Sarason 1981; Rose-Krasnor 1997; Silbereisen 1995; Welsh & Biermann 2001; Schoon 2009). Thus, we follow the modell by Stanat and Kunter (2001) in describing the skills which lead to social competencies:

- *Cognitive abilities* such as taking up other peoples' perspectives and self-efficacy;
- *emotional and motivational factors* such as self-regulation, respect, appreciation, empathy, and social orientation;
- observing *norms* or keeping promises and giving assurances;
- *value-oriented attitudes* towards assuming responsibility, violence, tolerance, participation, convictions related to justice and attitudes towards minorities (cf. the overview in table 1).

Table 1: Skills to social competencies

	Cognitive aspects	Emotional and motivational aspects	Value-oriented attitudes
In relation to oneself	• Attitudes concerning social self-efficacy • Language competencies etc.	• Self-regulation competencies • Respect and appreciation etc.	• Assuming responsibility for oneself • Attitudes towards violence • Tolerance etc.
In relation to others	• Taking up different perspectives • Competencies in decoding languages and emotions etc.	• Empathy • Social orientations • Objectives of social behaviour • Respect and appreciation etc.	• Taking responsibility for others • Attitudes towards violence • Tolerance • Attitudes towards participation, democracy and sustainability • Attitudes towards minorities etc.

Source: Inspired by Stanat & Kunter 2001

Raising self-efficacy and self-concept

Crucial for the training of social competencies in schools is to raise self-efficacy. As explained above, the cognitive aspects of social learning relate to oneself as well as others. Crucial to social learning is the belief that one can be a socially effective human being. This conviction of social "self-efficacy" is a central aspect of the core social competencies. People experience themselves as socially effective when they're given an opportunity to make experiences and have the possibility to assign the result of these experiences to their own behaviour. Activities which lead to positive results are crucial for raising self-efficacy and self-concept.

The American psychologist Bandura (Bandura 1997; cf. Fuchs 2005) identified four different experiences in this regard:

- Mastery-experience: Success in handling a difficult situation strengthens the trust in our ability to handle complicated ones in future. Failure creates doubts about our skills and leads us to avoid difficult situations in future. Thus, people who have a degree of high self-efficacy continue despite setbacks.
- Vicarious experience: If individuals with abilities similar to our own can overcome difficulties, we tend to believe we can master them too. However if those individuals fail, we too will lose our motivation to even try. The more similarity we finds in the behaviour of others like us, the more we'll be influenced by the outcome of their experiences.
- Verbal persuasion: Individuals who receive supportive and encouraging words that they can master a particular situation will try harder to do so. They believe more strongly in themselves than those who doubt their abilities. At the same time, it is important not to demand too much from someone as failure would cause them to lose their motivation.
- Stress reduction: Too many demands placed on individuals produce stress, strain, tiredness and/or fear. The person can easily interpret these negative feelings as weakness, thus creating self-doubt. Reducing stress helps people face challenges in a more relaxed manner and ultimately master them.

On one hand, communication in school and in extra-school settings can contribute to increased self-efficacy and self-concept. Likewise, it can systematically weaken adolescents' trust in their own self-efficacy. Other factors that reduce students' self-esteem include: poorly trained teachers who themselves have low self-esteem; high social selectivity in the school system; uncomfortable physical or emotional settings for social interactions (i.e. a communication style geared more for an army base than in a class room); human rights violations in school (i.e. public humiliation or corporal punishment). A supportive complimentary communication style that challenges and encourages students, teachers who themselves are role models for positive interaction and who communicate effectively on the subject of the lesson and exactly what will be taught help improve the students' sense of self-efficacy. Lessons geared to strengthening the pupils' self-efficacy of pupils change the teacher's role in the classroom (see Fuchs 2005). The learning process is no longer designed as a one-size-fits-all training course, but rather challenges each pupil individually according to his/her learning stage, thus catering to the students' diverse needs and the heterogeneity in class. The teacher is no longer an agent for selection by blaming students, giving marks and looking for mistakes, but supports pupils socially by giving positive feed-back, looking to learning processes and organizing the support between the learners. Teachers become positive behavioural role models and with guidance from the teacher, students can also become positive behavioural role models for one another. The teacher's role does no longer lead to pupils being stressed. The teacher organizes learning processes in a way that learning without stress but with concentration becomes possible

Experiences from PAP in Rwanda: Changing the role of teachers
Crucial of PAP in Rwanda was to change the role of teachers in class. Teacher trainings focussed first on the understanding of classroom-organisation in regard to diversity and individualisation. Teachers learned a lot of methods in the classroom to enable students' activities, to give feedback and therefore to enable students having experiences of self-efficacy and raising self-esteem. Individual working allows mastery experiences. Teacher learnt to overcome their concepts of discipline, obedience, and homogenous mass-education in order to focus on individual expression, learning experiences and reflectivity.

Another component to raise self-concept and self-efficacy is language competency or the ability to translate emotions into language. Decoding emotions and, in particular, working on language and discursive negotiations plays a major role as well to use positive emotions as stimulus for oneself and for others. The translation of emotions into language is a challenge. A detailed knowledge of a language is required to express emotions in that language. This presents a challenge since in many countries people's mother tongue and the language of communication (lingua franca) are different. This demands greater learning effort and carries the added risk that the social aspects of the language disappear due to the emphasis placed on factual linguistic expression.

1 Social Competencies, Learner-Centred Education and Peace

> **Experiences from PAP in Rwanda: The promotion of language and communication competency**
> One priority of the PAP courses in Rwanda concerns the participants' language and communication competency. Teachers learn systematically to increase their range of expression and create content from different perspectives. Examples include "the mirror" exercise, I-messages training, and active listening exercises (cf. Grêt 2009, 67 ff.). Basic aspects of communication theories are presented, such as constructivism or the dependency on the perspectives of those communicating).

The realization that one's own world view is subjective and not universal because other people can perceive the same facts quite differently is crucial to achieving social competency. This arises from knowing that knowledge is produced in each person's mind and a personal construction (cf. Glasersfeld 1989; Meyer 2009; Taylor 1998). Taking into account one's own perspective, the perspectives of others and the ability to change between them is central to social education. This change of perspectives can take place within the classroom if the lessons are organized in a way that different perspectives can be expressed without sanctions. It's important to present multiple perspectives on topics in school lessons, for example in history and social sciences. Multiperspectivity is also relevant when presenting various solutions for mathematical problems, discussing hypotheses in natural sciences or interpreting works of art.

> **Experiences from PAP in Rwanda: Group work and multiperspectivity**
> Group work in class is an important component of PAP training. Teachers are trained to organize group work so each student is involved and responsibilities are shared. This ensures students contribute instead of trying to hide within a group or blithely accepting the group leader's opinion out of laziness.

Value attitudes and social competencies

Social competencies are also passed on by the value-based attitudes of a school community (see table 1). A crucial point is the assumption of responsibility: Do teachers assume responsibility? Do they care about others and serve as positive role models? Do the school and its teachers reflect the main societal values with regard to good governance? Is corruption eliminated? Are examinations conducted properly? What attitudes concerning violence are evident in daily school life? Do teachers succeed in minimizing and eliminating violence? Does school discipline evolve on the basis of agreements and rules that resemble formal contracts – similar to those in modern societies? What attitudes towards tolerance are passed on in school? How are minorities treated and how do people speak about them? What sort of attitudes becomes visible in this area? What is tolerated in school lessons and what is unacceptable? What attitudes towards democracy are expressed in lessons? How are aspects of democracy taught? Are microforms of democracy practiced in lessons? This includes providing space to discuss conflicts in the classroom and working on them through constructive discussion.

Trauma and social learning

Trauma can only be addressed by educational measures to a very limited extent. Psychological concepts dealing with trauma emphasize the importance of participation and the strengthening of the self-esteem (cf. Fleischhauer 2008; Scherg 2003; Mehreteab 2002). Schools could make an important contribution with regard to students who experience traumatic situations, but schools must also look for outside support and encourage psychological experts to work with traumatized pupils individually.

> **Experiences from Rwanda: Dealing with mourning and trauma**
>
> The wars that occurred in the country and region since 1990 and the Rwandan genocide in 1994 left important traces among Rwandans. Many people suffered from serious emotional as well as physical injuries. They experienced psychological trauma, as well as social and relational problems. Some continue to suffer even today.
>
> Often, the PAP trainings were – and still are – the first opportunity for teachers to deal with these issues. Within the safe confines of the seminar, teachers could speak freely on a voluntary basis and enjoyed the sense of belonging to a group, In addition, the sensitively chaired seminar, the content of the training and opportunities for self-reflection all combined to create the space for teachers to deal with their own pain. The notion of mourning is crucial since many people, especially teachers, were affected by or participated in the massacres during the wars and genocide. The different phases of mourning are discussed during the PAP training and teachers can choose to discuss and interpret their own mourning using the concept of the different phases of mourning. Many gratefully availed themselves of the opportunity. It cannot substitute for psychological trauma counselling

but nonetheless facilitates open communication and provides emotional relief. Through the experience, many teachers realize for the first time that they need professional support to deal with their trauma. In the first years of PAP training, an expert on traumatic experiences held sessions during the seminar in order to train teachers, as well as the trainers and principals, how to handle a situation where traumatic outbursts occur.

Social competencies in globalising times

To meet the challenges of today's accelerated global social change, social competencies are much more necessary as in former times. In the face of an uncertain future, it's become increasingly important to develop personal and social skills dealing with uncertainty. The Delors Report to the UNESCO (1996) progress to greater personal development and individual empowerment. According to Jacques Delors, two of the "four pillars of education" should be dedicated to its social dimension. He posits "learning to live together" by "developing an understanding of other people and an appreciation of interdependence – carrying out joint projects and learning to manage conflicts – in a spirit of respect for the values of pluralism, mutual understanding and peace" (Delors 1996, 35). Learning to live together is inextricably linked to the second "pillar" "learning to be"…"so as better to develop one's personality and be able to act with ever greater autonomy, judgment and personal responsibility. In that connection, education must not disregard any aspect of a person's potential: memory, reasoning, aesthetic sense, physical capacities and communication skills" (ibd.).

In 2000 the Organisation for Economic Cooperation and Development (OECD) referred to the general learning requirements of Delors in a discussion of competencies during its project on *"Definitions and Selection of Competencies" (DeSeCo)* (Rychen & Salganik 2001). This project focused on "What competencies do we need for a successful life and a well-functioning society?" (ibd.) With this in mind, balancing conflicting requirements in an increasingly globalized world society becomes crucial: "Globalisation and modernisation are creating an increasingly diverse and interconnected world. To make sense of and function well in this world, individuals need to master changing technologies and to make sense of large amounts of available information. They also face collective challenges as societies – such as balancing economic growth with environmental sustainability, and prosperity with social equity. In these contexts, the competencies that individuals need to meet their goals have become more complex, requiring more than the mastery of certain narrowly defined skills." (Ibd., 4). The DeSeCo study identifies three key competencies: using tools interactively, interacting in heterogeneous groups, and acting autonomously.

The last two DeSeCo competencies are reminiscent of Delor's conceptual framework in regard to social learning. "Interacting in heterogeneous groups" is characterized as "the ability to relate well to others" (including the competencies of empathy and effectively managing emotions), "the ability to cooperate" (including the competencies of listening, negotiating constructively and coming to decisions) and the "ability to manage and resolve conflicts" (relating to the competencies of reframing conflicts and prioritizing needs and goals) (Delors 1996, 35).

Education must confront these competencies intentionally, especially in difficult social or post-conflict situations. Trying to impart these competencies is often described as "social learning", "democratic education" or "peace education". We also use this terminology, but understand these terms in their broader sense, as used by the OECD as competency-oriented dimensions. Self-concept, independence, the ability to cooperate and self-regulation skills signify core attitudes and psychological patterns that need to be promoted (Wang et al. 1993). These attitudes are not only supported by the content of learning processes, but in particular by the mode of communication during learning, allowing participation and empowerment (cf. Gillies 2007). By organizing the social climate of the learning process, expectations towards societal demanded behaviour are implicitly communicated and passed on. Therefore, these social competencies are essential and tightly linked to the behaviour of teachers. Quality of education is highly bound to the dimension of social interaction in learning processes.

1.4 Social Competencies and Peace in Society

Social competencies and societal contract

How social competencies are now related to peace and democracy in society? Social competencies are expected to increase social cohesion and minimize social conflicts. Societies become peacefully, if they achieve internal cohesion. In the family, genetic relations insure cohesion among individual family members. In (democratic) societies, the social contract performs this function. The

1 Social Competencies, Learner-Centred Education and Peace

resultant legitimized relations between individual members of a society, as well as the monopoly on the use of force to the state which, in reverse, is to control. Beyond the abstract relationship between state and citizens, the social contract must animate an appropriate welfare system, security, and mutual solidarity, primarily in the areas of health care, care for the elderly, investment in education and public goods (as water, sustainability, forests etc.). This remembers that enhancing social competencies in schools may contribute to better social cohesion but the impact will increase as much as the society itself is changing and welfare as security are provided. And in addition, a society's social cohesion does not derive only from the fact of its prosperity, but also that this prosperity is framed in a democratic context. This allows all citizens equal access to goods and conflict negotiation. Council of Europe policy highlights the fact that, in contrast to family cohesion, societal coherence doesn't come naturally. Societal cohesion can be influenced, i.e. strengthened or weakened, by the general political framework of the government and the civil society.

Even if education cannot ensure a social contract and social cohesion, it may support by enabling social competencies and – by this – higher personal autonomy. The Council of Europe emphasizes "that the achievement of social cohesion also has to centre on actively managing differences and divisions in a context of democratic citizenship. This is the bridge-building element. [...] This highlights a policy approach that actively seeks to prevent, negotiate and manage tensions, divisions and conflicts (relating to resource distribution as well as identity)." (Council of Europe 2008, 14; cf. Gaventa & Barrett 2010, 44) Educating social competencies is directly linked to dealing with tensions, and to respect the plurality of individuals. Learning social competencies is a key to learn how to deal peacefully with cultural plurality, migration and diversity through social competencies. Participation in education, an often underestimated aspect, imparts experiences in democracy which is essential cohesion. While teaching and enhancing social competencies, schools provide examples of appropriate social behaviour in social institutions while at the same time promoting this behaviour. The consequences of violating or disrupting a social organization can become visible (White 1998, 4). Strengthening social cohesion within a society by education could become an enormous force for change, especially in African countries with their large number of young people and increasing population. If social cohesion cannot be established, potential tensions might arise if the young generation can't participate in development processes or is denied access to it.

An appropriate education policy should guarantee access to educational institutions on the basis of equal rights and avoid exclusion. Education underpins the vision of learning as a means to improve an individual's living conditions.

> **Experiences from PAP: Giving space to different perspectives**
>
> The PAP training program in Rwanda emphasizes enabling teachers to manage their lessons so that pupils get an opportunity to introduce their perspective into the lesson. This can occur during partner and group work or via research for homework or solving mathematical problems in class.

The influence of social cohesion organized by the school system toward economic growth

These values even may enhance economic growth. In a 2000 study, Stephen P. Heynemann compared the university systems of former Soviet Union states with those in the United States, and argued that that "social cohesion has significant economic benefits; that since its invention in the 17th century, public education has been one of the main contributions to social cohesion in the west" (Heynemann 2000, 173). An educational system has a particular impact on the social cohesion of a society because: it constitutes public knowledge about the need for societal contracts; it organizes discussions about what social behavior is required for living together in society; it shows the consequences committing an offense against or violating the social contract (cf. Heynemann 2000, 175). The social capital that constitutes social cohesion will be secured by: 1) providing equal access to the educational system; 2) creating a consensus about the meaning of citizenship and common history; 3) organizing schools in a democratic and non-discriminatory way; and 4) providing assistance when different opinions about the first three conditions arise (cf. Heynemann 2000, 177). All these "make government, the economy and the national community work better". (ibd.)

Promoting social cohesion doesn't mean that conflicts don't occur or aren't allowed. Society is structured around opposing interests and conflicts are inevitable. They key is learning to deal with them in a way that strengthens social cohesion. This can happen when conflicts are seen as learning opportunities and as stimuli for further development of society.

1 Social Competencies, Learner-Centred Education and Peace

Social competencies and dealing with conflicts in society

To achieve social competencies does not mean that there will be no more conflicts in society. The essential is that people learn to deal with conflicts in a constructive manner. In everyday language, the term "conflict" usually carries a negative connotation. Conflict refers to any disruption to the lives of people (cf. Bonacker & Imbusch 2006, 67). Conflicts exist at all levels of human interaction: intrapersonal, interpersonal, intra-societal and international (cf. Bonacker & Imbusch 2006, 69; Pfetsch 1994, 213). Generally speaking, conflicts can be defined as a "communicated disagreement". (Luhmann 1984, 530) A conflict exists "if expectations are communicated and the non-acceptance of the communication has been fed back" (Luhmann 1984, 530; translation A.S.). According to this definition, conflicts represent a form of communication and the issue becomes how to deal with and settle them. Thus, expectations are an important driving force of societal differentiation; they simultaneously create complexity and present a solution to handling it. Learning social competencies represents the most constructive tool for dealing with complexity.

Therefore it is crucial, how individuals, groups, societies, and countries can organize their communication in ways that allow for conflict mediation, and use the conflicts as a means of contributing productively to the future development of all parties involved. Moreover, mechanisms must be developed to end violent conflicts or prevent them from arising in the first place. Education has an important role to play in achieving this goal. Through "learning by doing" and "exemplary learning", students learn how to solve conflicts through language and inclusion with the help of symbolic acts. In addition, in their role as a social organization schools can show their students how such organizations function.

As mentioned above, social cohesion doesn't mean that conflicts won't occur; indeed due to the structure of society, conflicts are inevitable. Schools are often expected to contribute to the post-conflict reconciliation process, create peace among the conflicting parties and provide a perspective for successful life (cf. Singh 2003; Lange 2003). School education can foster attitudes based on mutual respect, shared interests and common values, thus helping to underpin social cohesion in culturally diverse societies. Likewise, it can promulgate ideas and practices that weaken cohesion (cf. UNESCO 2011, 160). For schools to contribute to developing peaceful societies, they must offer a peaceful environment for the students.

1 Social Competencies, Learner-Centred Education and Peace

The direct role of education in preventing armed conflict and helping to rebuild post-conflict societies has been widely ignored. While there is no simple relationship between what happens in schools and the susceptibility of societies to armed conflict, neglect increases the risk of a return to violence. For example, if education is not linked to opportunities in the labour market, aspiring to greater educational access can be a disappointing and frustrating experience leading to "white collar unemployment" (cf. Anderson 1999; Seitz 2004; 2006; Sommers 2010). If education is working with corporal punishment, this facilitates the use of violence in society.

Jean-Baptiste Ndamukunda, teacher trainer:
Discipline and positive pedagogy

Traditional education in Rwanda emphasized enforcing discipline by severe punishment. Parents and the administration accepted that the teacher wields total power over his/her students. I remember when I was in 3rd grade primary school my teacher hit me with a piece of wood because I didn't do a math problem. Barely able to walk properly, I arrived at home and told my parents what had happened. They couldn't believe their ears, yet told me the teacher only wanted the best for his/her students. Teachers assumed the role of parents. Many didn't have bad intentions but their actions were often uncontrolled.

Teachers were respected and sometimes parents would even turn to them when they had difficulties with their children at home. The teachers' sometimes violent responses lead to kids abandoning school, and contributed to students' lack of self-development and failure. The teacher would not only hit students who misbehaved in class with a stick, but also those who couldn't answer a question correctly. This is why some people still believe that students cannot achieve anything without corporal punishment.

Fortunately, corporal punishment has been officially banished from schools. Still, cases are reported where it still occurs. During PAP training, teachers are helped to change their attitudes towards corporal punishment and create a positive environment in class. Violence against students is never a solution.

1.5 Social Competencies, Learner-Centred Education and Educational Quality

Social competencies and educational quality

Strengthening social competencies and self-esteem is not only strengthening social cohesion in society but to enhance school performance, thus raising the quality of education. Now that access to education has improved thanks to the "Education for All" programs of the Unites Nations, the focus of education debates in Africa in coming years will shift to improving educational quality (e.g. Avalos 2003; Riddel 2008; Verspoor 2008). In politically fragile situations educational quality is be seen as a stabilizing factor and given even more importance (e.g. Retamal & Aedo-Richmond 1998; Tawil & Harley 2004; Davies 2004; Smith & Vaux 2003). Improving social competencies is tightly linked to better educational quality, which can be achieved by raising knowledge, supporting resilience, and promoting self-regulation and self-efficacy. Recent research indicates the impact of participatory teaching methods impacts learning outcomes and the sustainability of the lesson topics more than the teacher's charisma or personality (cf. for higher education Deslauriers et al. 2011; Seale 2010). Often raising social competencies and raising self-efficacy is summarized as "learner-centred education" (see for Namibia Storeng 2001). Why are social relations, social competencies and self-efficacy so relevant to educational quality?

Self-esteem and academic achievement

The close correlation between academic achievement and academic self-confidence has been proven in numerous studies (cf. summarizing Zeinz 2006). Self-esteem and self-esteem strengthens academic achievement and vice versa (cf. Moschner 2001, 632; Krupitschka 1990). This interrelationship shapes the students' confidence in their own abilities, causing expectations of success to raise or fall, which affects ambition and aspiration levels. It also influences the learner's decision on how much effort, ambition and persistence to invest in future school assignments. Paralleling the development of self-esteem from different sub-areas, Hattie (1992) showed how not only academic self-concept but also social, emotional, and physical self-concepts all play important roles in academic achievement. Helmke (1992) discussed how at the start of performing a task, self-esteem influences the outcome, while during the consolidation phase self-esteem is influenced by routine achievements. Negative self-esteem often leads to avoiding tasks with little perceived guarantee of success, thus increasing the negative disconnect between self-concept and achievement. On the other hand, optimistic self-esteem can propel achievement (Helmke 1992) and indirectly helps future efforts (cf. Martschinke & Frank 2002, 192). These relationships indicate how the feedback process between academic achievement and self-concept proceeds in both directions and influence each other mutually.

Lessons design to enhance positive self-concepts

How can lesson design influence the development of a positive self-concept? An important factor is the range of *freedom* offered to students in class. Positive self-esteem increases in self-reliant students while the negative linkage between low self-esteem and academic achievement begins to dissolve. The teacher's common reference orientation also influences student's self-esteem. Negative self-esteem reduced in classes where teachers have as reference orientation to look after each individual student (cf. Kammermeyer & Martschinke 2003).

A second factor is to see learning as an *emotional task*. Emotions help fine-tune the learning experience because of their importance in cognition (cf. detailed Damasio 1994; Roth 2001; school: Scheunpflug 2001; Scheunpflug 2006). (cf. Roth 2001, 258). Emotions have evolved throughout the history of mankind and everyone's emotions are based on the same physiological foundation. Failure and success are crucial to learning. The brain has its own internal system of reward (in detail Roth 2001, 297 ff.), that engages when a situation turns out better than expected. The brain's own reward system depends less on external attributions of success than on an individual's subjective evaluation of his/her expectation of success. It supports academic learning if the school's expectations lie slightly higher than the level a student could achieve without effort. Challenges should be designed so as to be achieved with minimal effort. This reward system becomes problematic when conditions are unclear or tasks are unachievable. Then, hormonal reactions push the student to abandon efforts and a vicious circle of failure ensues. The internal system of reward is controlled by one's own expectations, which don't always correspond with external perspectives on success and failure. Positive emotions arise in situations where expectations can be achieved, not in indifferent situations or those with no expectation of success. A positive stimulating environment is most likely to provide the internal evaluation that creates interest and desire to learn.

The third aspect is to organize lessons in a way that they *allow flow and creative passion* processes. Mihály Csíkszentmihályi has been researching this topic since the mid-1970s (cf. Csíkszentmihályi 2000). Known by those in the progressive movement as "creative passion" by Kurt Hahn or "polarization of attention" by Maria Montessori, Csíkszentmihályi's mechanism posits that concentrating on a task is easier and more satisfying if the effort required correlates with one's abilities. Then one doesn't get bored or overwhelmed and the necessary effort engenders a feeling of self-efficacy. That only occurs when feedback on the solution of the task is given. The sense of losing track of time while working, being focused and using the released energy to devote oneself to the task at hand seemingly without effort is termed "flow." Against this backdrop, the conditions for creating a flow experience that facilitates learning are given when there is a balance between outside demands and the student's own abilities, marked by a recognizable yet manageable challenge. The task objectives should be clearly and precisely phrased and feedback should be immediate. Whenever possible, the student should be able to influence the task by action (e.g. by choosing the degree of difficulty or, ideally, by defining the task itself).

Forth aspect is to be conscious about how to organize *comparison* in class. People often compare themselves to others to get a sense of their own strengths – whether in cognitive performance, social behaviour or overall self-esteem. This comparison occurs automatically, though schools invite comparison by virtue of grades, praise and reproach. Basically, comparison occurs in three distinct ways:

- The "individual reference norm" compares a person's current achievement against a previous one, thus indicating any changes in performance.
- The "social reference norm" compares and ranks one's own achievement against the achievements of others.
- The "criteria reference norm" compares one's own achievement vis-à-vis the desired objectives of the task. What has and hasn't been achieved becomes apparent.

Being aware of these three reference norms and dealing transparently with them in class is an important step in strengthening self-esteem. Students must be told what they need to know and do academically so they can perform to the highest level. They need to know the criteria established by the teacher in order to perform effectively. The individual reference norm should always be made transparent by the teacher. This type of class practice will be presented in chapters 2 and 3.

How students understand their *success or failure* is the fifths important aspect of learning and acquiring self-esteem. People divide into two groups: those confident of achieving success and those who focus on avoiding failure. Success-confident people attribute success to internal causes and failure to time-variable factors, factors which can change with time. Thus, when successful, they experience the positive effects of self-evaluation. When they fail, they might feel bad, but the possibility of succeeding next time remains due to the assumed time variability. People who avoid failure often attribute success to external causes, and failure to time-stable, constant factors, especially their own limited abilities. Thus, even when failure avoiders succeed, they derive little pleasure from their performance; when they fail they become anxious and their hope for better performance in future declines. Success-confident people tend to set realistic objectives and choose intermediate-level tasks, whereas failure avoiders set unrealistic goals, often choosing tasks which are either too easy or too hard.

Dealing favourably with success and failure in a way that adds to self-esteem can be learned. Underachieving students must be made to deeply understand that they can improve their achievement level. The teacher must be convinced that performance and behaviour can change and be able to convey this to their students (cf. Dresel & Ziegler 2006).

The sixth aspect is to understand *mistakes as a learning resource*. How teachers handle mistakes in class is important. For example, mistakes in a trial test or during a class conversation could be interpreted as inadequacy or a failure to learn a topic. However, mistakes also can be seen as an integral part of the learning process that fulfils an important function. Mistakes point the way to learning how to do something differently or better next time. They also highlight areas where specific assistance can be useful. The challenge for schools is to close the gap between interpreting mistakes as a starting point for assistance and using mistakes as the basis of performance assessment (see chap. 2).

Furthermore, in order to experience themselves as efficient, content and self-confident, students must *believe they can increase* their abilities. These "implicit theories of capability" are closely related to the students' experience of themselves in school. If teachers can help students understand that they're capable of increasing their abilities, they're very likely to work more intensively. Empowering students by believing in their success is an important aspect of being a teacher.

And last, the *climate of interaction in class and in school* is important. School climate is shaped by interactions and relationships such as: manners, opportunities for participation, types of conflict management, the emotional quality of relationships. In abstract terms, school climate can be defined as "communication relations, role self-conception and sensitivities of groups involved in school" (Eder 2006, 627). Research on school climate reveals that "students with positive climate experiences show higher participation in class, disturb less and therewith create better conditions for learning and achievement" (ibid., 626). Positive climate arise in tandem with positive social interaction, and are often linked to a smaller academic burden (fear of school, stress) and a positive (achievement) self-concept and self-esteem (cf. ibid.). Positive climate experiences can help students develop their potential.

Summary: Understanding the mechanism of learning

Fig. 2 summarizes the major assertions of the "learning engine" concept as the basic mechanism of learning.

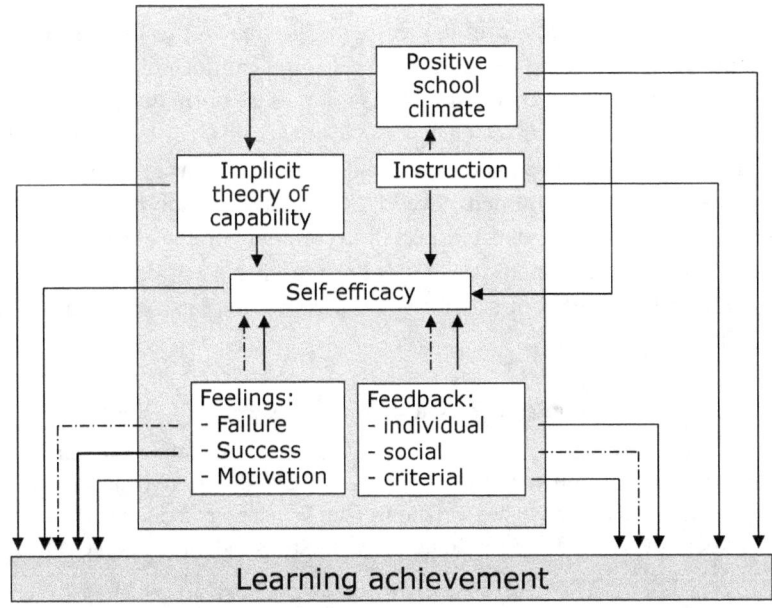

Fig. 2: Understanding the Mechanism of Learning (Source: Zeinz & Scheunpflug 2010, inspired by Helmke 2010). Solid line = positive reinforcement, broken line = negative reinforcement.

Learning achievement is the fundamental goal of all school efforts. It depends on interactions among the various influences as shown above. These include a positive school and class climate and the students' belief in their ability to influence/change their competencies. Good teaching benefits this objective, especially because of its positive impact on self-esteem. Emotions relating to dealing with failure, success exert both positive and negative influences on self-esteem, as does comparing one's own achievement. Success encourages learning, failure hinders it. Individual and criterial comparisons also encourage learning, while social comparison usually operates against it. Only one person can be the best, albeit temporarily, and second place is sometimes considered as defeat.

Interaction and positive feedback

One of the main challenges to improving education is enhancing the interaction between teachers and students at all levels (see for Africa Yu 2007; Stanat et al. 2010). As the focus of these educational efforts, students must above all receive adequate feedback from the teachers. "Feedback" means a response to every behaviour or academic performance. "One cannot not communicate", writes Watzlawik. Even ignoring a behaviour or performance constitutes a response. The word "feedback" has come to mean an intentional rather than an unintentional response to behaviour and is used more as constructive criticism. In a learning environment, "feedback" was traditionally reserved for the teacher. Nowadays, students are expected to comment on the performance and behaviour of their classmates as well as their teacher. Positive and encouraging feedback is of great importance when it comes to constructing a positive self-concept.

> **Experiences from Rwanda: Increased student self-esteem**
>
> The traditional Rwandese concept of teaching devoted a lot of time to teacher explanations and demonstrations in front of passive students. Students responded only reluctantly and rarely asked questions. They were often afraid of speaking in class because they didn't want to show any weakness and thus provoke violent responses from the teacher.
>
> Their fear was also due to students who habitually booed and humiliated classmates who didn't succeed instead of encouraging them. In this teaching method, mistakes are not allowed.

In contrast, PAP encourages students to express themselves, discover new subjects, interact with fellow students (especially during group work), and make presentations in front of others. During our follow-up visits, we watched students proudly presenting their results to others, whereas before they'd never wanted to talk or share their work. The pride associated with actively participating and contributing to the deeper discovery of a subject creates self-esteem among the learners and affirms his/her personality and existence among other people. Learners feel strong and don't despair when confronted with difficulties.

During the practical week of PAP, a student in a primary school ventured that it was the first time he ever felt happy in class after presenting his group's results at the blackboard to the acclaim of his classmates who previously considered him a "goof."

The long road from knowledge to practice

Teachers must learn these new approaches to teaching (cf. Tschannen-Moran et al. 1998). Teaching and learning are social activities based on patterns of self-understanding and social roles. Social competencies can only be learned through practice, not merely by knowledge transfer. Improving core social competencies represents a challenge for the education system at all levels and not only for the students but leadership, principals, teachers and teacher trainers, as they all serve as examples to their students by their own social competencies and determine the social climate. Motivating and training teachers is therefore a crucially important issue.

Some complain that it takes too long for teachers to integrate the content of the training courses into daily school life. However, changes to lessons that directly address attitudes and values are strongly connected to the teachers' own values and attitudes. Values are relatively stable and cannot be changed from one day to the next. It takes time to reorient values, a supportive climate to test out new patterns and sufficient financial support. Sometimes expectations of instant change are too high after a relatively short training course. In order to change attitudes and values about social cohesion, the trainings must be long enough to build confidence in the respective groups of participants (see chapter 2).

1.6 Conclusion: Social Competencies and Self-Efficacy as Learner-Centred Educational Responses in a Post-Conflict Society

The central idea of this chapter is that building self-esteem and a positive self-concept, as well as strengthening social competencies such as changing perspectives, empathy and sensitive language constitute the core of a pedagogy that responds adequately to post-conflict situations and incorporates social learning, peace education and learner-centred education approaches. Theoretical foundations for this thesis are presented and illustrated with experience from a program from Rwanda. This type of pedagogy

- frees up students and teachers to use these tools constructively in class;
- represents a method of instituting democratic experiences and social participation;
- enhances learning conditions and teaching quality;
- is an adequate response to post-conflict situations, especially when wounds are still fresh and critical examination of events hasn't yet taken place;
- contributes to a culture of peace and social cohesion in society;
- establishes a culture of self-regulation, responsibility for students and teachers, enabling them to make their own decisions and
- encourages the individuality and self-regulation necessary in modern societies.

Strengthening social competencies in class as well as strengthening self-esteem and self-confidence improves teaching quality because:

- The students' "learning engine" is supported and learning becomes noticeably more efficient.
- The targeted feedback about their performance that students receive enhances their learning performance.
- Students participate in class more actively and express their own individuality more. Student heterogeneity is accepted and encouraged.

The experiences presented in this book represent a contribution to learner-centred education. How such an approach works and how it can be implemented will be presented in detail in chapter 2.

1 Social Competencies, Learner-Centred Education and Peace

Religious perspective on education for responsible freedom

The approach to peace- and post-conflict education presented in this book was developed in Protestant schools. Of course this approach is not based on any religion. Nonetheless it takes up two central perspectives of Protestantism:

Firstly, Protestant education should always be subject-oriented. Subject-oriented education is "the meaningful demand from man to comply with his purpose as God's creation in aspects and relations beyond social standardization and short-term instrumentalizations" (EKD 2010, 14). From a reformation perspective, the likeness and personhood of each individual person before God is being emphasized. As God's representative on earth, the individual is perceived as capable of and trusted with autonomous judgment concerning theological and other questions regarding other dimensions of life. God's gracious and merciful devotion to humans bestows autonomy and responsibility upon them. Committing to God's commandments gives humans the "Freedom of a Christian" (Martin Luther), which releases them from many constraints and renders them open to turn to their neighbour and assuming responsibility for fellow humans and for society.

Pedagogy accompanies adolescents on their path to maturity, autonomy, and responsibility. For theological reasons, education should strengthen the student's own activities and responsibility. "A Protestant profile arises where young people are potentially enabled to experience the comfort and the demand of the gospel and where they can fathom out the meaning of the freedom of a Christian in their own lives" (EKD 2010, 14).

Secondly, the aim of all educational efforts results from the basic principle of serving the wellbeing and salvation of all people, or biblically speaking, the "Shalom". Where "mercy and truth are met together, righteousness and peace have kissed each other"(Psalm 85.11), the prophetic vision of a renewed and changed world through God's shalom can be experienced today. Martin Luther urged schools to contribute to "peace, justice and life." Because young people are guided by education towards a behaviour promoting peace and justice, Luther's dictum requires an educational component.

1 Social Competencies, Learner-Centred Education and Peace

François Rwambonera: PAP and Protestant Churches in Rwanda

Ever since Protestant churches were established in Rwanda at the beginning of the 20th century, their activities have focused on three pillars: evangelization, education, and health. The three complementary pillars underpin a person's holistic development. The Protestant churches in Rwanda pushed forward an educational vision of simultaneously instilling the good qualities of a worker as well as a citizen. Thus in addition to creating primary schools, the churches created vocational training centres for boys (construction, carpentry, etc.) and girls (nursing, sewing, cooking, etc.), pedagogical schools, and later, secondary schools for general, technical and vocational teaching.

According to the churches, schools weren't merely settings for acquiring knowledge and competencies. They were also places for students to acquire, internalize, and express the social and Christian values characterized by a Protestant education as integrity, love for God and your neighbour, justice and peace, patience and humility, property, truth, and spirit of responsibility, creativity and entrepreneurship. However when social context changed after the 1994 genocide, the Protestant churches understood that this new context required new educational behaviour and attitudes. It called for active and participatory teaching methods to foster understanding and social cohesion and to create a climate of understanding. The Protestant churches recognized PAP as a means to answer the challenges. Since then, the field has grown considerably; by 2011/2012, the Protestant churches maintained more than 1,000 schools with almost 10,000 teachers to train.

The new pedagogy within the Rwandan school system instituted by the Protestant churches was very popular with public and private stakeholders in the education sector. Practicing PAP not only supports and improves learning; it also helps to implant a culture of peace that manifests in socially harmonious and respectful relationships. These relationships evolve in a climate of play, self-development and trust. They are maintained and preserved through positive, supportive and secure environment. The Protestant churches in Rwanda have 15 years of experience practicing PAP. The process wasn't always easy, especially as the entire socioeconomic sector had to be rebuilt. Initially the teachers felt physically, morally and psychologically insecure. Many had lived in refugee camps before joining the trainings. Despite the difficult times, the Protestant churches believed in the approach and persisted. Offering spaces for prayers, meditation and spiritual needs was also important, not just for personal reasons but also as a way to deal with mourning and as a source for reconciliation and developing new perspectives.

The Protestant churches still face the constant challenge of training more teachers in PAP to augment the number of teachers trained so far.

2   Teaching Social Competencies

What are the main aspects to draw attention on in applying a participatory and active pedagogy or learner-centered education in post-conflict situations? What would be the main components and methods of such an approach?[1] *This chapter addresses these issues, looking at content, methodology, classroom-management and its interplay. A lot of these issues are known as crucial for instruction and in a lot of cases there are already used. What is new for PAP is to use them consequently, to focus on communication and activity, and to adopt them to the situation in the country.*

2.1   Content: Through Students' Eyes

PAP is focusing on social competencies. This affects the organization of the content to be learned.

Clarity of content

To concentrate on communication and interaction does not mean not reflect the content. It's the opposite – the more the students have the possibility to interact and to communicate, the more the content to be thought class must be reflected by the teacher. The German educator Hartmut von Hentig's has put a lot of emphasis on this aspect by saying "To clarify things, to strengthen people" (v. Hentig 1985). Students enjoy class if they feel they're advancing in learning knew knowledge and are frustrated if they feel inadequate to deal

---

[1] UNESCO and the United Nations have a lot of material on peace education (for example Fountain/UNICEF 1995; UNESCO 2001; Office of the High Commissioner for Human Rights 2003; see chapter 2), but few reports deal with experiences by practitioners in situ. Conley Tyler et al. from the International Conflict Resolution Centre at the University of Melbourne, Australia, developed a peace education curriculum for Vietnamese primary schools, including a teachers' manual (Conley Tyler et al. 2008). Using the UNESCO 'peace keys' as adapted from the Manifesto 2000 (UNESCO 2000) and other materials, they designed a five-year peace education course with 50 lessons. In addition to the content, they incorporated physical group activities, games and reflective activities. Harris (2004) identified five types of peace education: international education, human rights education, development education, environmental education and conflict resolution education.

with. To teach knowledge correctly and clarity of things to be taught must be the foundation of a participatory and active pedagogy. Given that teachers do not have in a lot of cases a good formation and therefore lack of knowledge, writing the objectives on the blackboard and making them transparent, is a chance to let the students take their responsibility to for the clarity of what should be thought.

> **Experiences from PAP in Rwanda:**
> **Adequate knowledge and clarity of objectives**
> In order to focus on clarity of content, teachers defined the contents of the class before the lesson and were trained to write the lessons' objectives on the blackboard at the beginning of class. To know what is have to be done gives students guidelines for reference throughout the day. If students lose touch during the lesson, having clearly defined content and objectives enables them to orient themselves. Both teachers and students benefit as it's easy to return to the topic after student questions or other distractions.

Linking knowledge in classroom to the real world

It is crucial for PAP that students link the content to the world in which they live and their own inner world. New knowledge may only be acquired by creating a link between the new concept and something already familiar to the student. Creating these connections is one of the central challenges for participatory and active pedagogy. There are different possibilities to link new concepts to existing ones; one important way to do so is to seek for connectivity to the students' living environment. The philosopher Edmund Husserl defines "living environment" as the natural everyday environment. Strengthening the links to the students' living environment means addressing issues in class related to political changes, religious or spiritual questions, topics that impact the students' future (i.e. vocational training, employment, subsistence.) Students will assimilate new curriculum topics more easily if they can relate them to their daily environment. Teachers can choose math problems that involve calculating costs of building one's own company or interests on credits, etc. Natural sciences topics could relate to the function of solar watches and solar power or the biological processes during the reproduction. Language instruction could involve producing short newspaper articles or local radio reports. Strengthening the link to the students' living environment also means including parents, the community and the local authorities in curricular activities and involving the school in the local community and municipality by letting students participate in maintaining public buildings, sustainable projects or taking care of the elderly.

Experiences from PAP: Positive communication

Positive, polite communication can help create positive social interactions. Kinyarwanda is the mother tongue in Rwanda, but official and school communications have been taken place in French and now in English. The ability to communicate politely in the official languages creates opportunities in later professional life and also engenders positive feelings and among people.

Students in the English class were split into small groups of six or seven, with each group receiving a poster with a number of English expressions. The groups developed sketches representing everyday situations wherein the expressions on the posters were used in polite and positive communication. Examples included excusing themselves for coming home late; being invited to a friend's place for dinner, going out on a first date. The groups performed their sketches in front of the class and received feedback from the teacher and their classmates. The classmates had to identify the polite expressions the group had used in their sketches. Afterwards the posters were put up on the wall.

In post-conflict situations, the students' environment is often characterized by war-related events and creating links to this painful past is difficult. Great sensitively is required to avoid flash-backs or rekindling traumatic experiences and to balance difficult political situations.

Experiences from Rwanda:
Failing in balancing political situations in PAP text book

One program in Rwanda emphasized participatory learning in history class. The government of Rwanda took part a joint consultation with Facing History and Ourselves (FHAO), the University of California Berkeley School of Education and Human Rights Center to develop a History Resource book "Teaching History of Rwanda: A Participatory Approach for Secondary Schools" (NCDC 2005). The PAP-book has not yet been disseminated (cf. Rutayisire 2007, 121; Rutayisire et al. 2004; Obura 2003; Obura & Bird 2009; for the writing process Freedmann et al. 2008) as it did not see appropriate to the authorities fearing not to weaken the political concept of unity in the country by enhancing individual expressions and positions towards history.

Linking learning to the students' environment implies developing didactic materials from that environment. Stones or fruit might be used as visual aids for math calculations; wall posters could be made from drawings on paper or cardboard; garbage or found objects could be used as scientific models (i.e. communicating pipes made from plastic bottles).

> **Experiences from PAP: Working with didactic material**
>
> To help motivate teachers produce their own materials, didactic materials for various subjects were developed during the PAP training using objects found in the environment. In PAP schools, important concepts like the world map or the human skeleton are painted on school walls so students can constantly see and refer to them.

Linking to already learned aspects

Student attendance in post-conflict situations can be irregular. In this situation, as well as in normal cases, topics to be learned must be linked to previously learned topics so that the process of building progressively on knowledge can occur. Learning problems and exam failures arise when new content hasn't been adequately assimilated because the previously imparted content wasn't fully understood.

Learner-centered education and participatory and active pedagogy therefore imply creating links to prior knowledge. Teachers must be able to diagnose problems when dealing with students' learning disabilities so they can ascertain why a student isn't mastering certain content and help them fill in the gaps.

> **Experiences from Cameroon: Chaining content**
>
> The Dynamisation Fonctionelle de la Pédagogie/Functional Revitalization of Teaching, (DYFOP) teacher training project in Cameroon consciously used curriculum modules that built upon one another. The modules contained tables of natural science and math problems that students needed to solve in order to progress with these subjects. In this way, teachers' diagnostic abilities were honed and they had adequate tools for pinpointing their students' learning difficulties (cf. Scheunpflug et al. 2011; Bergmueller et al. 2012).

Awareness of not-knowing

In today's knowledge society, knowledge has become an important resource. Students need to learn this. They also must learn that knowledge is produced by people and can always be expanded upon. Likewise, any increase in knowledge involves a simultaneous increase in ignorance. In other words, the more you know, the less you know!

A learner-focused orientation and participatory and active pedagogy can be used to track the development of knowledge as well as showing that part of knowledge means dealing constructively with *not* knowing. Post-conflict situations are often characterized by authoritarian structures wherein an authority figure feigns knowledge and ignorance or questioning is not at all seen as appropriate. In such a culture, teachers set themselves up as primary repositories of knowledge. Admitting to not knowing something and learning strategies to acquire knowledge are important aspects of participatory and active pedagogy and learner-centered education.

Experiences from PAP in Rwanda: Dealing with not knowing

Many teachers told us how PAP changed their teaching methods as well as their attitudes toward teaching. Before the training, most felt they knew everything and their students knew nothing. If they didn't know something, it didn't exist. After PAP training, teachers felt okay about not knowing everything. They now consider themselves as partners in their students' learning process and understand this means acknowledging they don't have all the answers. Together with their students, the teachers develop ways of acquiring knowledge such as interviewing people in the community, going to the school library, or – when possible – using the internet.

Competency orientation

Competency orientation is a style of teaching in which the aim is acquiring knowledge and learning to apply it in different situations. In a lot of situation in development countries or post-conflict countries, knowledge is learned, which is never even asked to be applied. To teach competencies means to teach in a way, that things are already applied in different situations in the classroom itself. Competency also includes motivational aspects: It means linking capabilities of finding solutions to problems with the motivation to face challenges: "According to this definition, competency is a disposition that enables people to successfully solve particular types of problems, that is to deal with certain kinds of concrete situations" (Artelt & Riecke-Baulecke 2004, 27; cf. Klieme 2004) It deals with the ability to face complex challenges in a specific situation (Rychen & Salganik 2003, 2). Subject-related competencies contain the classical competencies of knowledge, understanding and judgment. The aim is to know facts, rules and terms; to understand phenomena and arguments and to learn how to assess different situations. This competency is often imparted implicitly when dealing with different topics in class. Methodological competency includes abilities such as excerpting, looking up something, structuring, planning, designing, visualizing, or working independently on complex tasks. In class both aspects – subject-related competencies as well as methodological competencies – should be addressed. In addition, imparting competencies is means not only to focus on testable knowledge, but on acquiring abilities *relevant* to problem solving.

Applying knowledge demands self-reliance on the part of the students, since they're the only ones who can solve the problems. Competencies can be described at different levels. Therewith, students can be individually supported by going from one level to another.

Focusing on competencies underpins students' sense of the self-reliance. It also implies that:

- The *culture of class* exercises must be changed. Instead of routine exercises, students must learn how to transfer what they've learned in other areas to the current problems. They must also learn how to apply problem-solving thinking to new learning situations.
- Lessons must be changed so that students can become *agents* of their own learning.
- *Individual support* in the classroom must occupy an important role.
- In the method of *dealing with mistakes* in class must change so that mistakes are seen as natural to the learning process and an important stepping stone for further learning.

Experiences from PAP: Focus on transfer
Teachers trained in PAP don't only focus on knowledge but have been trained to help their students acquire competencies. They accomplish this by providing time for reflection either individually or in groups. They make time for inquiry and research, during which the students seek to solve problems. Thus, the students develop a culture of inquiry and learn to take responsibility for their own learning.

During the lesson, teachers give students the opportunity to link what they've learned with situations in their everyday life. They're asked identify topics in other disciplines where the current lesson content could be applied to solve a problem. They either do this in class or as a homework assignment, with results presented later. This is what is called "generalization" in the course of the preparation of the lesson.

Sustainability as an important Issue

Participatory and active pedagogy also deals with topics relating to students' futures as to be addressed in the context of education for sustainable development. Education for sustainable development meets "the needs of the present without compromising the ability of future generations to meet their own needs" (Brundtland World Commission 1987, 24). The notion of sustainable development was taken up and specific measures put forth as an issue for all parts of society in the AGENDA 21 of the United Nations Conference on Environment and Development in Rio 1992. Education for sustainable development promotes a balanced and integrative approach to environmental and development policies, to cope with current and future challenges of the world society (cf. Agenda 21 1992, 1). The demands of the younger generation in terms a worth living perspective are focused.

Experiences from PAP in Rwanda: Protecting the environment

The primary school of Banda is located close to the Nyungwe Forest national park. Half of its teachers were trained in PAP in 2005. After the school implemented the new approach, various extra-curricular clubs started on topics such as anti-AIDS, reconciliation and peace and the environment. The "Environment Care Club" was initially formed to care for school property, but later extended its activities to the forest and the surrounding community. Its goals were to protect the local environment while simultaneously creating awareness and mobilizing the local community. The club planted trees and reached out to the community with theater performances, poems, dances, and posters.

The local authorities became aware of the students' commitment and visited the club several times. They invited the club to participate in national competitions for environmental protection, at which the school won several trophies.

Thanks to PAP, the students became more active, creative and assumed greater responsibility.

To promote sustainability, its objective must be shared and supported by a wide segment of the population. Education for sustainability is a guiding principle that can be adjusted according to the ecologic, economic and cultural backgrounds of a given situation. Economic and ecological sustainability needs the cooperation and support of all citizens, therefore involving everyone's participation. To achieve sustainability individual interests, those of coming generations have to be balanced. Against this background, core social competencies are an indispensable part of education for sustainable development. Empirical research shows that education for sustainable development contributes to social learning processes and the experience of participation (cf. Rode 2005; de Haan 2010).

2.2 Methods: Cognitive Activation

Functions of activating during lessons

Activating methods in class are a key element of participatory and active pedagogy. Activating students may have three different functions: students may be sensitized to a subject by activities, they may explore or elaborate a topic or they may discuss and work on transfer of knowledge (cf. Scheunpflug & Schröck 2003).

Sensitization is often related to start with a topic on mobilizing the students' ideas, prior knowledge and attitudes. The more the students can relate a topic to their own experiences, the more active, creative, and communicative they'll be and the more open to learning. Brainstorming, picture associations, producing mind maps, judging and justifying theses are useful methods.

Exploring and *elaborating* means that the students work on factual information to describe problems, estimate consequences, analyze causes and backgrounds, and develop solution strategies. Crucial learning activities include: research, text analysis, expert interviews, debating the pros and cons, designing posters and wall newspapers, producing or solving crossword puzzles, passing through a learning circle, etc. These activities support target-oriented information exploration and enhance the students' methodological, social, and personal competence. Initial problems become more easily identifiable and new questions arise.

In regard to *problematisation and transfer*, topics associated with the students' learning activities and new knowledge can be addressed. A pro and con debate format, a hearing or conference game (in which the roles of people involved in decision making process are explored), help develop the students' abilities and their readiness to become involved. Presenting results can also open the door to new questions and areas of discussion. Creative methods are needed so the teacher's "chalk and talk" doesn't become the students' "chalk and talk".

Experiences from PAP: Giving space in structuring and giving lessons

A PAP lesson is part of a dynamic progression. A good lesson must draw on what's already been addressed, yet al.so allow for developing new concepts which can be applied to future lessons.

In contrast, traditional lesson preparation in Rwanda contained certain steps to which the teacher must adhere absolutely. These include: the annual, trimestrial, weekly, and daily progression (the sequence of chapters); the division of preparation sheets must be maintained (revision, introduction, the lesson itself and application). In Rwanda, a teacher must follow these steps to the letter. In the traditional teaching methodology, teachers followed the pre-established lesson plans from the educational authorities to the letter. In PAP the lesson is part of a chapter which in turn is part of program designed to function at a specific level. A structure of domains and themes generally exists for all classes, but in PAP this structure is dynamic, not static. PAP permits creativity in structuring the lesson during the preparation as well as the execution phase.

Teaching methods for activation[2]

Mapping opinions and attitudes: "Mapping Opinions" is a method to highlight various opinions and attitudes. It takes place in small group which provides a safe space where opinions can be articulated without being aired in the plenary. A statement is written on a poster or on the blackboard, i.e. "Girls should stay at home and help with the household"; "I think I understand the Pythagorean theorem." Students decide whether they agree/disagree or understand/don't understand. The teacher hang on one side in the classroom a card indicating "I agree"/ "I understand" on the other side one "I don't agree,"/ "I don't understand". Students indicate their "standpoint" by positioning themselves between the two cards depending on the level of agreement. In small groups than students discuss their agreement or non-agreement, or those who understood will explain those

---

2 The following examples are partly drawn from Scheunpflug & Schröck 2003.

who did not understand. In this process they learn to argue, justify their position, learn to be tolerant of other's opinions, and learn to explain by their own.

Card Query Method: This card query method helps to structure a topic. Students receive an initial stimulus, for example: "When I think about community development, I think of …." They respond by writing keywords on a piece of paper. Dividing into small groups, students present their ideas and agree on 3 to 5 keywords which are noted on individual cards. These cards are presented to the other groups by explaining and pinning them on a wall or blackboard. Then they are clustered according to topics. These cards than may use as guidelines for deepening topics, for discussions or questions.

This guided individual work motivates all students to actively deal with the subject. During group work, individual thoughts need to be presented and the group needs to agree in the end. Too reach an agreement, they need to discuss and make compromises. A presentation in the mentioned way prevents that the last group doesn't have anything to say anymore because everything has already been mentioned by the previous groups.

Judging and Discussing Statements: Statements discussion is a method for fast and communicative introduction of a topic. The students receive a worksheet with different thesis which they need to rate according to a scale from +2 ("I totally agree") to -2 (I totally reject"). The students discuss their ratings in small groups. The speaker of the group then briefly presents the course of the discussion in the plenary: Where was a consensus, where were differences? To prepare a statement for the plenary asks for a deepening content-wise. Presenting in front of the class supports self-confidence and communicative competence.

"Sayings Course": The teacher collects sayings to a respective topic and writes each on an individual paper. The papers are hung up on the walls, leaving sufficient space between. According to the number of papers, groups meet in front of a paper, and discuss the following questions:

1. Describe the saying! What does it express?
2. Which problem is addressed?
3. Which are your experiences with that problem?

The results are noted. Groups have 3 to 5 minutes for each paper; then they move clock-wise to the next station where they repeat the procedure. In the same way, quotations, short texts and pictures can be worked on.

Working with texts: Texts are a dominating resource in class. The common way of text interpretation isn't very inspiring for students: The teacher sets tasks or asks questions, the students read the text and answer the questions. Interpreting text in a rather uncommon way does not only provide variety but also promotes the students' self-reliance and creativity. One possibility is, i.e. to transform text in a differing format as:

- Doing a fictive interview with a person occurring in the text or writing a letter to the persons occurring in the text or their friends. If one has already experienced a situation as described in the text, a letter could be written to a friend or to the parents, too.
- Writing a report for the student newspaper with texts, illustrations and commentary. If a student newspaper doesn't exist, the title-page of a fictive subject-oriented newspaper could be produced.
- Producing a three minute radio spot with news, interviews, commentary, music etc.
- Initiating a talk at a congress regarding the subject of the text (including a short role-play in class)
- Creating a comic to the text.

Information in the text may be analysed by producing a crossword puzzle. Working with literary texts, *pictures* or *posters* can be designed and produced which could be used as title-page. Producing posters about the content of a text may visibly integrate analyzed information in the classroom. At the same time, students learn an important working technique. A *mind map* is a form of presentation which can bring structure to texts and thoughts. Connections and aspects of a topic are recognizable at a glance. Mind-mapping is a creative working activity which corresponds with the network structure of our thinking. Using mind maps in class, e.g. when exploring the influences of the weather on the crop, students not only learn intensively about content, but are trained in an important key qualifications: dealing with complexity.

Group- and partner work: To split the class in smaller groups, working together or working in pairs, activates all students at the same time. "Group Puzzles" are a method, to intensify the work in class, when students work on different aspects of a topic in small groups. After exploring their aspect of the topic, groups are mixed in a way that each of the former groups is now represented in the new groups with at least one "expert" for every topic. The experts inform the other members about his/her topic. Producing a learning poster ensures that connections are established between the different aspects of the topic and gives to the teacher the possibility to control the learning process.

Projects: One of the most known methods of a longer lasting method is project work. Implementing projects in class should open up spaces of action to students and therewith promote self-reliance and self-determination. Meyer describes a project as "an attempt by teachers, students, included parents, experts etc. to connect living, learning and working in a way that [...] a topic or problem chosen by the teacher can be dealt with inside and outside the classroom" (Meyer 1987, 143 f.). Regarding its realization however, this working form is "so utopian that sacrifices when implementing it in class are inevitable" (Meyer 1987, 338). But even with these, projects represent a top form of students' self-reliant learning. They are one of the most challenging forms of pedagogical action. Students need to have the methodological competence to productively learn under their own control.

These preconditions are rarely given. Projects in class are often used as stopgap to bridge the last weeks of school. Whether projects, in regard to their expected learning outcome, might then even be counterproductive is an open question. A number of well prepared modules on a topic are often more effective than a project in class which overwhelms the participants.

Research: Research can be used to promote the methodological competence of dealing with knowledge and information. Starting from the school library, from the local church, the market or from authorities, different topics can be researched. When heading to institutions outside the school, it needs to be sure that there is an adequate contact person for the students.

Pros and Cons Debate: As in class it is not naturally given, that students see the pro and cons of a topic and are able to debate, it might be helpful to cultivate these arguments in a way, that one students get the "pro" position, another the "cons" position, they prepare for arguing (may be in groups) and then start the debate. This enhances the quality of argumentation and debating in class.

Future Workshop: The method of the "future workshop" should enable students to systematically and constructively deal with a future-related topic. During the first phase, optimistic utopias are developed out of wishes and dreams. After a second phase, in which the current situation is criticized, the develop utopias are reviewed against the difficulties of realizing them. A future workshop gives many opportunities to deal with the question how students want to shape the future. In future workshops, future is understood as something can be actively and self-responsively shaped. Future workshops are characterized by a composition of different methods into a method combination. Including playful and creative elements, creativity techniques as well as shifts from single presentation to discussion, group work and work in the plenary, future workshops allow learning which emphasizes possibility to shape a humane future (cf. Jungk& Müllert 1998; Weinbrenner & Häcker 1991).

Methods for presentation of results

Activating learning and working methods need corresponding methods of presentation. If one group representative after the other presents their results, the students' attentiveness drops continuously. The groups' results don't reach the classmates. Working methods which allow the presentations to be more fascinating and lead to discussions among students are described below:

Role plays: Role plays support the students' ability to change perspectives and find solution to problems or conflicts. The separate scenes should only last a few minutes. This description partly follows Fountain (1996, 11).

- The frame and the roles need to be described in detail while still leaving space for personal interpretation.
- All students need some minutes to think about their role.
- Name tags facilitate keeping a distance to oneself and ease entering into the new role.
- The spectators don't comment during the play.
- The spectators take notes about actions which change the course of the play. Why was a solution found? Why this one and not a different one?
- The role play ends when a solution is found, when the scene takes too long, or when the players have difficulties to stay in their roles.
- After the play, the players have the opportunity to express their feelings during the play. Are they happy with how it ended? The spectators give their impressions and propose alternatives.

Variations of role play may allow deeper reflections:
- During an intense moment of the role play, the teacher can suddenly call out "Freeze". The role play becomes a freeze image. The players describe their feelings in this moment.
- The teacher stops the role play without warning. The players change roles and continue the play from that point.
- An observer stands behind each player. Halfway through the role play, it is stopped and the observers say what – according to them – their corresponding player feels and thinks at that moment.

Fish Bowl: Like in a fish bowl, the group representatives sit in a circle in the middle of class. The teacher or a student leads and hosts the discussion. One empty chair is put in the middle of the circle. The classmates follow the discussion from outside the circle. There is no strict succession of the arguments. Who wants to respond, add or reject to what another group representative has said, may immediately do so. Students from outside the circle can join the discussion by taking the empty chair and expressing their argument. Afterwards they leave the circle again.

Double Circle (Ball Bearing): Students form an inner and an outer circle, sitting face to face to each other. They have three to five minutes to present and discuss their results. After this time, the outer circle moves on (clockwise) one or two chairs and another exchange can start.

The Gallery: Learning posters, mind maps or other products are put up on the wall. Like in a gallery, students pass from one exhibit to the next, examining the results, noting remarks or writing on an empty poster next to the exhibit, prepared beforehand by the teacher.

Relay presentation: The first group presents and explains their results. The second group briefly reacts to the results of the first group. What impressed them, what was well done? Did group one set a different focus than one's own group? Etc. The next group proceeds the same way. Each group always starts with occupying itself with the previous groups' product. After the last group, the first group acknowledges its product.

Expert Interview: External experts can add new and further aspects to a topic. Preparing such an interview (e.g. phrasing questions) students are required to intensively engage themselves in the topic.

Gérard Ugirashebuja, secondary school teacher:
Learning about Napoleon

While dealing with French history, the name of Napoleon came up. As the students didn't know who he was, I as a teacher set the following task: Go into the community and interview people. Find out what they know about Napoleon. The next day the students came back and reported the following: Napoleon was a French general who fought in wars. Now they were motivated to learn about him as they knew that this knowledge has some relevance.

2 Teaching Social Competencies

Félicité Musabyemariya, primary school teacher:
Dealing with heterogeneity

Musoni, a 38-year-old man, had left school many years ago. After the national politics made entering schools easier, he came to take up his primary school education again. He was put in class with 7- to 12-year-olds where he finished his primary education. Thanks to PAP, he was well integrated in class despite his old age. At the beginning it was difficult, as the little children made fun of him. But step by step he became part of the class and the children got used to him due to the practice of PAP.

Just as Musoni, many people, especially teenagers, went back to school to finish their education. We accepted seven students. Among those applying where orphans, people who had left school due to family problems or the use of corporal punishment in their former schools. Using PAP, the students experienced an inviting school, where students are motivated and encouraged, where teachers talk to their students to learn about their different family and social situations. Considering the personal backgrounds of students is important for organizing the learning process as different people need different things.

Thanks to PAP, the school has become very successful in the academic competitions on regional level. And among the most successful students we find those, who had left school but then returned after a certain time to take up their studies again».

Marlène Mukandoli, primary school teacher:
From teacher-centered teaching to learner-centered teaching

Before the training in PAP, the teaching was focused on me. In my 4th grade primary class, I presented the topic and the children only listened, read and copied notes. My students were passive and the results were fair. A third of the class failed the exam. Using active methods, it's no longer individualism which rules, but cooperation. I introduce the lesson, after which my students and I explore the didactical material which I prepare in advance. I give them detailed instructions and they work actively in their groups.

Each group works indefatigable to reach good results. A spirit of listening is developed among my students, respect of the other, and flexibility. The successful atmosphere has raised among them a taste for school and learning. I have a class which is open, motivated, flexible, and which easily processes the topics.

After some time, I changed schools. In my new school, PAP wasn't known. It was and still is the traditional pedagogy which leads to frustration, harassment, failure, inhibition of initiatives and creativity, etc.

> I started to introduce PAP in my class. My students seemed shy at the beginning, but because I created good working conditions, they opened up little by little, they thrived, they talked, they discussed among themselves. They like the way I work. They brag about it in front of the other kids in school. They work better, they succeed. I hope that all my students will succeed at the end of the year and move on to the next class.

2.3 Classroom Management: Empowerment and Recognition

A person's self-esteem is dependent on the recognition by others. Participatory and active pedagogy assumes the recognition of the other. Recognition is understood as an attitude of respect towards other people with needs, opinions and interests, which is unattached to the other's achievement or function relevant to oneself. Axel Honneth states that recognition is the basis of a value-oriented interpersonal contact. The „Struggle for Recognition" (Honneth 1992) shows the „moral grammar for social conflicts" – to show the students respect takes them out of this struggle and opens up spaces for the development of young people. It relieves social stress. This relief is especially necessary in post-conflict situations while at the same time it is hard to achieve. Recognition is also influenced by the image of humanity, which becomes visible in the whole of all interaction of a person. Generally speaking, every interaction between teachers and students should be rooted in the mutual recognition of everybody's dignity. Additionally, a central category of recognition is to see the adolescent as learner. Essentially, each young person wants to learn. Even if this may not find its adequate representation in the adolescents' everyday activities, it is a question of mutual recognition and respect that this is assumed by the teacher. The recognition of the other as learner defines the educational relationship and the educational consideration.

Recognizing somebody is expressed in respectful social interaction characterized as follows: active listening and letting others express themselves, being open to others' ideas and needs, seeing something from the perspective of the other's thoughts and feelings, patience and confidence in the fact that one will understand the other better with more time and more information, and the trust that one can explain him/herself when feeling misunderstood. Joachim Kahlert, professor of pedagogy, explains: „Recognition cannot be operationalized by a catalogue of rigid behavior demands. It is the attitude to respectfully allow the other to have rights and needs which is crucial. […] If recognition is the right everybody can make use of, then attentiveness towards the other is the corresponding obligation with which the right can be secured as far as possible for everybody." (Kahlert 2010, 9)

Capitolina Nyirabazamanza, primary school teacher: Empowering students

Before the formation in PAP in 1999, I couldn't lose time taking care of the weak students but with the good ones. After the training I started helping the weak students to improve and had to realize that it was only my weak judgment which had kept the students from succeeding and performing miracles.

In 2004, a girl from a neighboring school came to repeat the 6th grade with me. Her former teachers told me how stupid she was and that she should rather leave school and get married. I believed them and thought for myself that she was only going to waste her time. But when I realized that she actively participated in class, I paid more attention to her, asked her to present the results of her group and tried to establish a feeling of success. The girl became more active, the shyness and frustration disappeared and at the end of the year, she finished 3rd out of 36. She succeeded in the state exam and moved on to secondary school. Her former teachers as well as her parents came to school not only to thank me but also to learn more about this new pedagogical approach which had let to such a miracle.

Recognition, in reverse, doesn't mean that one necessarily has to accept what the other is doing: "Taking up an attitude of recognition, one doesn't have to accept all social impositions of the other's behavior. As the freedom of one stops where the freedom of the other is wrongfully restricted, such reaches the realization of the right to recognition its limits when it disproportionally compromises the other's right to recognition." (Kahlert 2010, 9)

Especially during the dispute about social behavior and in the feedback to inappropriate social behavior, recognition towards the other is shown, as there is no higher form of recognizing people than others dealing with them.

Possible connections to educational practice already become visible. From this perspective it is apparent that to perceive students in school in all their facets is important. Recognition also shows when the living environment of certain students is being apprehended by their class community.

Césarie Uwabaganwa, primary school teacher: PAP reinforces sociability
One of my students in 6th grade lost his father. Some of the students and teachers went to the funeral. The next day, the dean of the school summoned the 6th grade students and told them about the problem of their classmate. They decided to collect some money to visit him, each one according to his/her possibility. While the students collected the money, the dean came and told me about this, asking me permission to join. I informed the other class teachers of the 6th grade so that we could also participate. After one week, they had collected 6000 francs (about 8 EUR). A small delegation including four students and me went to the family. It was a big surprise for the family and the kid showed his gratitude. He and his mother were very encouraged by this friendly gesture.

Abandoning corporal punishment

Participatory and active pedagogy and learner-centered education show themselves if an attentive and friendly climate prevails which abandons corporal punishment. Especially in post-conflict situations and in face of a general climate of violence, school often can't withdraw from an educational approach, in which corporal punishment is an everyday practice. As mentioned in chap. 1, school provides a bad example regarding social competences and social cohesion if they accept corporal punishment. But even if corporal punishment in school is officially prohibited, as is the case in Rwanda, it often stays everyday practice. Reason for this are often poorly trained teacher with little pedagogical competence who don't know how to act differently in their everyday teaching. Recognition is being also shown if students are assured of their physical integrity and if this human right is considered of high value within the school,

For this purpose a classroom management is needed which assesses social behavior through communication.

2 Teaching Social Competencies

Tips from practice: Dealing with interruption in class

Many teachers are faced with the problem that they only hold a poor repertoire of possible behaviors with little alternatives to easily abandon corporal punishment. PAP aims at developing a number of possibilities in dealing with interruptions in class. It is important to comprehend interruptions as students' signals needing to be individually-sensible interpreted – just as any other behavior. Such behavior has *causes* (constitutional factors, unsolved conflicts, interrupted development processes, and current threats) and *objectives* (apology, cover-up, arousal of attention, prevention of inferiority or gaining superiority, revenge, affection, prevention of boredom). The following list describes a number of possible behaviors:

- Consciously ignoring (not sensible with provocations)
- Utilizing signs (if they are known to correspond to certain rules, e.g. raising one's hand for silence after group work)
- Changing of the bodily distance
- Unobtrusive affective attention (eye contact, smiling ...)
- Relaxation through humor
- Helping to overcome an obstacle (against interruptions due to fear: encouraging, building bridges)
- Restructuring the situation (defamiliarizing when boredom prevails)
- Moving students (to de-irritate, not to label the disturber)
- Intellectual counterarguments (explaining, only if the joint aim is the search for truth)
- Getting aware of/removing emotional tensions
- Appealing (emphasizing the class interest against egoistic behavior)
- Argued restraints
- Rewards (as a sign of thank you and happiness)
- Threat (Not to frighten and intimidate the student but as a warning to protect the student!)
- Punishment (not to weaken the students' ego which would lead to fear and revenge, but as offering „re-socialization")

Source: Winkel 1996

Marlène Mukandoli primary school teacher:
No more corporal punishment

For many years, I terrorized students in my class with rude remarks and corporal punishment in order to correct their behavior. I wasn't happy about it but I didn't know how to act differently; and I thought it was normal to act that way. After my training, I systematically started to change my teaching. I started using I-messages, there was no need to club and I felt confident in organizing my lessons. I can see that this has led to better results:

- I have better relations with my students.
- Absenteeism has decreased.
- The dropout rates are lower.
- The class is more pleasant,
- My working environment is nicer.

Théophile Mutuyeyezu, primary school teacher:
Violence causing drop out

Dropout rates were very high in our school in all grades. As principal I interviewed the students concerned as well as their parents, many of whom mentioned that they were afraid of school and especially dreaded corporal punishment. Even though corporal punishment has been banned from our schools, it still exists. I therefore intensified the PAP training in our school. Gradually the conviction arises among colleagues that corporal punishment isn't an adequate educational tool. Some teachers started to feel embarrassed about their behavior and tried to win back students through personal dialogue.

Silas Nsengiyumva, primary school teacher:
No more corporal punishment

Before the training in PAP, I would hit students who were late without asking them why they were late. After some training sessions I decided to abandon this bad habit. I was touched a lot by some of the sessions such as the I-message, mourning, or rules for life in a group.

These topics gave me the opportunity to correct my students without hurting them. Instead of clubbing them, I now listen to them which have created a climate of trust, free expression and dialogue. Now, when a child arrives late, I ask the reason for his/her delay, I listen carefully, the students explains the reason and when he/she finishes, I judge the student together with the class representatives.

If there's a good reason, the student may take his place. If there isn't we relate to the rules of life in a group.

A girl from my class arrived late one morning. When I asked for a reason, she asked me to talk to me privately which I accepted. She told me she had to prepare food for her dad which was in prison. I felt touched and relieved because if I had hit this girl I would have only worsened her situation. I often rejoice at PAP because it has changed me and allowed me to abandon the use of corporal punishment.

Feedback

We already mentioned the function of positive feedback. Four different types of feedback can be distinguished (the following text passage is based on Scheunpflug et al. 2012, 53–55):

(1) Incorporated written feedback is normally done by questionnaires. These can address the school, the class, or a single lesson. Complete and tested questionnaires as well as question batteries which can be assembled according to need already exist for student feedback on class- or school-level. Question focus e.g. on the teacher-student-relation, the average quality and the required level of performance in class, or the climate in school. Questionnaires related to a single lesson address e.g. the comprehension of the subject, the interest in the topic, the requirement profile or the joy of learning.

(2) Open written feedbacks are especially suitable for classes who already have experiences in constructive student feedback. There are types which only allow for positive statements as an exercise in improving the class climate; e.g. each student can communicate something nice to another student or produce a sticker with a positive adjective for a person. Letters can be written to the teacher in which students can write what they like and what they don't like about class or what they wish for in the future.

(3) Closed oral feedback is based on systematic questions. These are either given by the teacher or are developed within the learning group. They can relate to the content (What do you know about the French Revolution?), the behavior (Which social behavior is beneficial to a positive class climate? Which behavior do I expect from the teacher?), to the lesson (How did I feel in class today?) or the times of group work (What supported and what prevented my participation). It is advisable to produce feedback rules, and display them well visible in the classroom (cf. Klippert 2009).

(4) *Open oral feedback* needs a trusting atmosphere in class as well as experiences with constructive feedback. The more open and unstructured the frame of the feedback is, the more influenced the feedback will be by the individual perceptions of the students. This is suggestive when students have sufficiently experienced feedback structures and when teachers are willing to embark on the students' perceptions.

> **Tips from practice: Possible rules for feedback in class**
> - Speak personally: Express "I-messages".
> - Describe, don't judge: Less "You didn't do this well", but: "I don't understand this part of your text".
> - Justify your feedback with arguments: "I see it this way, because …"
> - Start with positive feedback.
> - Be a precise as possible.
> - Explain consequences: Detailed explanation of further expectations for work.
> - If necessary immediately afterwards or later: Discuss possible activity options. (Who contributes what to success?)
>
> Source: Scheunpflug et al. 2012, 54

A common type of feedback is *grades*. Empirical studies in so-called industrialized nations have shown that over 40 percent of the students were dissatisfied with the assessment of their academic achievement in their mother tongue, Math, and the first foreign language (cf. Stadler-Altmann 2010). Reason for this is that learners usually can't comprehend the common assessment practice. It often rests unclear to them what a good grade is substantially composed of. For example, students with a low self-esteem often see good grades as a fluke. Students with a high self-esteem see a bad grade as a slip, even if it is based on serious topical shortcomings. Both attitudes can prevent consequent learning. Therefore a transparent grading with a clear feedback is important, in order to avoid misunderstandings underlying the students' attitudes.

> **Tip for practice: Transparent grading**
> - Students should have a *clear understanding about which performance is expected of them*. Competency frameworks or lists distributed in class, stating what needs to be learnt for example, can serve this aim.

- Feedback should *individually relate to the results*, e.g. demonstrating and acknowledging different solution possibilities for one and the same math exercise.
- *Grading* has to be solely oriented at *criteria of factual connection* (i.e. criteria references). The individual reference standard should be explained, if an improvement isn't (yet) to be seen in the grade.

Source: Scheunpflug et al. 2012, 55

Student self-reflection

Constructive feedback within participatory and active pedagogy also means that students learn to give themselves feedback and to reflect upon their own behavior or their own learning progress. Learning should lead from dependency to independence. Learners need to learn to develop their own (academic) goals. They need to learn to verbalize their goals and ideas. When verbalizing they develop an inner picture of what should be developed. Different maps exist which contribute to students' self-reflection (cf. Müller 2008; Müller & Noirjean 2007; Scheunpflug et al. 2012, 47):

- *Competency framework:* Competency frameworks are used for putting educational requirements in a synoptic scheme. They are organized in tabular form: On the vertical line, criteria are mentioned which define a subject or competence content-wise (What?). On the horizontal line, each criterion is defined by four to six competence levels with increasing and succeeding complexity (How well?). Competence frameworks can show possible horizons of development. One's own abilities are described in a differentiated way. Therewith, learners receive the possibility to realize their own competencies and to position themselves. As each students starts at his/her own initial point, there's the possibility to define individually adequate goals. Competency frameworks are oriented towards standards as they are established in curricula for example.
- *Checklists:* While competency frameworks summarily summarize requirements, checklists structure the differentiated everyday work. Checklists provide detailed information on what is meant by the competence descriptions. They function as personal learning and development plans due to their strategic selection.

- *Smarties:* Checklists are written as "smarties", as goals are supposed to be described "smart"ly. Smarties describe the expected result in a way that it is going to be sense perceivably manifested.

    S   Specific: What is it about (precise description of the topic)?
    M   Measurable: How do I know that I reached my objectives?
    A   Attainable: Can I reach my goal? What is to do, to reach it?
    R   Relevant: Which relation has the goal to my every-day activities?
    T   Time-bound: What should be done until when?

Teachers in Cameroon have positive experiences using such forms of self-reflection for students. They are collected in the students' exercise books and parents regularly need to sign them. It strengthens the students' self-efficacy and contributes to mutual clarity.

2.4 Linking these Elements in Program

Participatory and active pedagogy therefore also means that content, methods and the way in which those two interact in classroom-management need to be liked in a way that students are put at the center of attention. Often, these three elements can't be implemented at the same time. Therefore it might be advisable to emphasize on one element or the other in order to implement it in a situational adequate way.

> **Experiences from PAP: Objectives of the PAP program in Rwanda**
>
> The program underlying this book a strategic focus was set on positive communication. The PAP program tries to systematically strengthen the feeling of self-efficacy among teachers and students and contribute to social coherence and peace in society. Teachers should be instructed to become more aware of the students' social needs and to offer them more space for freedom in order to strengthen their self-esteem and to achieve more self-confidence. Additionally, it aims at creating a social climate and environment which promotes better learning and blooming of the students, reinforcing the teacher's role as a facilitator and organizer in the students' learning process. Changing the dynamics in class will also influence school life as such, hence principals and parents also need to be involved.

Therefore the program also aims the school management to become acquainted with participatory and active pedagogy in order to be more aware of these innovations and to support them. Additionally it aims at the promotion of a dynamic and participative interaction between the school and the parents in order to develop effective participation on both sides in the education of the children, and the resolution of identified or experienced challenges and/or problems like the rape of children, HIV/AIDS, reconciliation or national unity, etc.

The main objective of the program is to improve the quality of teaching by a) improving and/or reinforcing the teachers' professional educational capacities in order to increase qualitatively and quantitatively the impact of their performances/educational services and b) by changing the teachers' and students' attitudes and behavior to adopt and incarnate the attitudes and behavior related to human and social values such as

- Conviviality and collaboration among the teachers themselves, among teachers and students, and among the students themselves,
- A positive communication with the development of a spirit of listening to each other,
- The creation of a good atmosphere and a social harmony as well as a good working climate at school,
- Respect for the other as a human being, for his/her rights, his/her opinion, his/her self-fulfillment, etc.
- The creation of a climate of professional and social solidarity between the teachers,
- The development of a spirit of responsibility and initiative in finding solutions to the problems met, and
- A culture of research and the promotion of good work, which is quality work.

3 Implementing Social Competencies in Schools

In this chapter, the question how to implement trainings on learner-centred education is addressed. First, the teacher training is described in detail (chapter 3.1). To ensure the acceptance the training, it is important to get al.l stakeholders involved, including parents (chapter 3.2). As learner-centred education requires change of attitudes and teaching behaviour, training has to be supported by follow-up and supervision in the classroom (chapter 3.3). To run a certain quantity of trainings, the recruitment and training of multipliers becomes necessary (chapter 3.4). Finally, quality management of the trainings and financial and funding requirements are mentioned (chapter 3.5 and 3.6).

3.1 Teacher Training

The teacher's new role in learner-centred education

Focusing on conveying social competencies in school implies a change in the teacher's traditional role. Instead of being all-knowing conveyers of knowledge, teachers become facilitators and sometimes even partners in their students' learning process and quest for knowledge. They are learning guides and coaches.

To facilitate learning activities such as partner and group work, discussions, performing and evaluating role plays, writing texts etc., the teacher no longer interrogates students. Instead teachers ask appropriate questions and actively listen to the student's responses. Teachers no longer occupy centre stage in the classroom. They shift the focus off themselves to allow time and space for students to work self-dependently, argue, present and debate. Their primary task becomes designing programs that allow students to learn and work independently. As learning facilitators, teachers advise and coordinate, putting the subject matter and the students' relation to it at the core of the learning process.

As persons of authority, teachers are behavioural role models. During the implementation of a cooperative approach to teaching, students become role models as well. Both teachers and students depend on their experiences at school; hence it's important they treat one another with mutual respect.

Jean Bosco Ndimubanzi, secondary school teacher:
How I changed my attitudes

Before my PAP training, I prepared my lessons without considering the students' contributions during the lesson. I saw myself as the only source of knowledge. I taught them and they needed me. Anything I didn't know didn't exist.

After the training, my attitudes changed. I no longer ignore my students, either while preparing or implementing the lessons. My students now give impeccable examples. They succeed because they overflow with knowledge. Now I prepare my lessons so as to leave space for students' ideas that arise from their group work. I'm no longer the instructor, but rather a facilitator who guides them on their quest for knowledge. I help them summarize their ideas from the group work. My students do very well on the various exams because they've discovered and built up their knowledge on their own.

The need for teacher training

Changing the perception of the teacher's role is difficult, as many teachers have only experienced traditional notions of what teachers do, beginning with their own student days and throughout their careers. Yet training teachers is of paramount importance in order to achieve quality in the educational sector (cf. Leu & Price-Rom 2006; Avalos 2006; Lange et al. 2010; Tatto 2007). A consensus exists about the need to invest in professional training and further education for teachers (cf. UNESCO 2011a). However, little experience is available on how to train teachers in the area of value-based social competencies.

Designing lessons from a supportive and encouraging perspective requires a number of teaching skills. Adequate teacher training or additional training for working teachers is crucial in the South, and especially in post-conflict situations, where most teachers have received inadequate training.

Immaculée Mukantabana, teacher trainer:
How the I-message lead to changes in my family

My son used to come home late at night even though I told him not to. When I opened the door I was always angry and repeated the same questions: "Where were you?" "Do you think I'm a night guard?" "I work hard and need my rest." But nothing changed. I assaulted and threatened him. Our conflict went on for months. We both grew increasingly angry.

Then I started PAP training and began to reflect on the situation and started using I-messages which was very difficult at first. Instead of verbally attacking my son, I explained the consequences of his coming late and how I felt about it. Upon opening the door I told him: "I'm worried that bandits will attack you and throw you in a gorge." "It'll be too late and we won't be able to save you or call for help." "Only bandits go around at night and I'm afraid they'll harm you." "Also, I have a bad headache and I must get up early tomorrow. I'm afraid I won't be able to work well." Step by step, my son changed his behaviour. He started by telling what time he'd be home, then where he would be. Finally we agreed upon a time he should be home. Now he comes home two hours earlier than before!

Silas Nsengiyumva, primary school teacher:
PAP reinforced family cohesion

Before training in PAP, whenever my wife and I had problems, I'd sulk and sometimes not speak to her for days. We had avenues of communication. I always saw myself as the innocent victim and waited for her to change her mind.

During the training I realized I was living a conflict I couldn't handle. Different topics such as mourning or the I-message helped me adopt a more communicative style toward conflict resolution.

Now when there's a problem between us, I invite my wife to talk to me. We discuss and exchange views until we reach a consensus. If I see I'm wrong, I apologize. My wife does the same. We now take time to dialogue whenever we have a misunderstanding.

Changing teachers' social attitudes and competencies

Learner-centred education touches the teacher's values and his or her self-image of being a teacher. To abandon an authoritarian teaching style requires communication competencies and sometimes personal courage. Teachers in post-conflict situations have few role models for learning open communication. They often lack experience on how to solve problems through communication.

Therefore, and to effectively change teachers' attitudes and teach them to address social competencies in the classroom, teacher trainings must cover a variety of aspects:

- Cooperation and communication: Teacher training should provide talks, exercises, and reflection that show the efficiency of cooperation in the

classroom and give teachers the opportunity to experience cooperation and positive communication.
- Values and self-image: Values should be addressed. During the training, values and the individual self-image of being a teacher need to be reflected upon.
- Cognitive competencies; Teacher training should include exercises on polite language use, change of perspective, empathy and expression of one's feelings.
- Communication competencies are complex and not easy to achieve. Teachers need "protected areas" (e.g. exercises in a friendly group of teachers) where they can practice the newly acquired approaches before applying them in the classroom.

Trainings should give teachers the possibility to learn about the importance of social competencies in society as well as how to actively advocate and practice them. A teacher's competence is manifested by visible actions. The Organization for Economic Co-operation and Development (OECD) defines acting competence in a broad sense: "The theoretical construct of action competence comprehensively combines those intellectual abilities, content-specific knowledge, cognitive skills, domain-specific strategies, routines and subroutines, motivational tendencies, volitional control systems, personal value orientations, and social behaviours into a complex system. Together, this system specifies the prerequisites required to fulfil the demands of a particular professional position …" (Weinert 2001a, 51; cf. Weinert 2001b, 27 f.) This quote states clearly that the didactical structure and content of teacher training should focus on obtaining social competencies.

The relation between teachers' professionalism and social competencies

Developing social competencies affects all aspects of professionalism in teaching. Baumert & Kunter (2006) consider the following areas as core social competencies for teachers: (1) knowledge; (2) value commitment; (3) motivation and (4) professional self-regulation.

(1) Core social competencies of teachers cannot develop without different forms of knowledge. First of all, general pedagogical knowledge is needed. Many teachers use outdated learning theories, for example that giving pupils bad grades stimulates their performance. They don't know that negative self-es-

teem hampers motivation. Instead, learning should be explained through motivation theory, self-esteem, self-concept and feedback. Classroom management, i.e. organizing group work, requires general competencies in managing space, time and people. Secondly, teachers cannot structure lessons without understanding their content and subject matter, without reflecting how students construct knowledge and how they progress in their learning process. Managing lessons in a way that individual stages are integrated depends on clear structuring of the subject by the teacher. Therefore knowledge about the subject is the basis for teaching social competencies. Subject-related competencies help teachers organize lessons in a way that pupils learn to think independently.

(2) Changes in teaching towards a fostering perspective require learning support, social assistance and patience. Teacher behaviour becomes an example and, through individual assistance, classmates become examples as well. Attitudes towards democracy, universal respect and human rights are important components of social education.

(3) Professional teachers are motivated to know about other persons, to reflect on communication and to care about their students.

(4) Instruction is linked to emotion. Teachers need to remain emotionally adjusted. Within a classroom management that focuses on individuality, autonomy and social cohesion, teachers require self-regulation to deal with complex social interactions. Teachers must learn how to create and organize lessons that don't elicit mere rote responses from students.

Training content

What topics should be addressed in training for to realize the above-mentioned goals and help teachers permanently change their habits?

- *The relation between learning, society and social change:* The learning process in the teacher training should address the interactions between learning, society and social changes. Teachers can think about how the *social demands* of learning affect education and their role in the learning process. Therefore issues like the change of the society, the necessity of learning and knowledge ought to be addressed as well as how the social demands of learning affect education and the role of teachers in the learning process.
- *Complex understanding of the learning process:* Studying the motivational and psychological foundations of learning (such as the learning engine, the

- *Forstering the self-understanding of teachers:* Pedagogical concepts and empirical findings about teaching and classroom management enable teachers to translate their newfound knowledge into a challenging self-understanding.
- *Didactical methods:* Exploring the various methods of activating teaching, such as working with partners and groups, self-evaluation, competency frameworks etc. will help teachers to expand their didactical repertoire and adapt it to different topics and situations.
- *Communication skills:* Using role plays or in-class practice, teachers can address, test and routinize different forms of communication, such as giving useful feedback, sending I-messages or organizing clear and concise lessons.
- *Evaluation and assessment:* Teachers can learn how to evaluate lessons and assess student performance in a way that corresponds with the dialogical understanding of the learning process.
- *Subject-specific transfer:* Planning and realizing specific lessons in different subjects during the training, integrating participatory elements, enables teachers to practice linking their newly acquired knowledge and competences with their everyday teaching.
- *Didactical material:* During the training, teachers can learn how to develop and produce their own didactical material for illustration, such as wall newspapers, scientific models from garbage etc. It will help them to positively deal with missing resources and enhance their creative and pedagogical attitudes.

Experiences from PAP: The content of PAP teacher training

The basic PAP training which lasts three weeks (two weeks of theory followed by one week of in-class practice) focuses on the interaction between students and teachers. It addresses five themes that constitute the teaching/learning process: pedagogy, methodology, psycho-pedagogy, psychology and communication.

In the pedagogy unit, concepts of pedagogical thinking and different approaches to pedagogy are introduced. Participants learn about instruction, group dynamics and the learning process in general. This unit also includes the class practice in the third week.

The methodology unit introduces participants to methods such as brainstorming, working with spreadsheets, group work, using anecdotes, preparing tests. Teachers learn about the advantages and disadvantages of group work and participate in discussions to clarify any questions or concerns.

The pedagogy and methodology units focus on the learner-centred approach, targeting interaction within the classroom. The psycho-pedagogy unit is situated at the intersection of classroom and teacher professionalism. In regard to professionally handling classroom interaction, it addresses rules for successful living and working together as a group and strategies for creating a positive classroom climate but also questions of endurance, job design, coaching or perception in regard to professionally dealing with teachers' requirements.

The psychology unit focuses solely on the teacher. It includes exercises to raise teachers' self-image and better understand their role as teachers. It also includes aspects of emotional wellbeing or rather non-wellbeing, such as mobbing, mourning or burn-out.

The communication unit presents theories of communication, different methods of communicating and presenting, self-related ("I") messages and non-verbal communication.

The entire course program has been published (cf. Rwambonera 2000; Grêt 2009; MINEDUC & INWENT 2007; 2008).

Dealing with burnout

Post-conflict situations often lead to teachers being overwhelmed or experiencing burnout. Like many people in service-oriented professions, teachers are at high risk for burnout. The work has no formal ending because teachers get involved outside classroom situations. Additionally, the profession demands a high degree of self-discipline which not all teachers can achieve. In post-conflict situations, the professional and the personal conditions of living are even more demanding. Post-conflict situations present additional stress factors:

- Students' psychological stress influences the classroom climate as well as the learning process, thus raising the demands towards lessons' planning and therewith towards the teachers' professionalism.
- Teachers often experience stress within their own homes; family members are psychologically stressed from the trauma and mourning.

- Because of the precarious post-conflict economic situation, the teacher is often the family's sole breadwinner.
- People are also highly stressed by the still ongoing societal processes of reorganization and the occasional flaring of riots. This applies to students and teachers as well.
- Traumatic experiences hinder self-regulation and self-discipline which then leads to experiences of being overwhelmed.

Addressing and finding ways to deal with burnout is an important component of teacher trainings. Not acknowledging the teachers difficult personal situation only adds to a teacher's personal burden.

Silas Nsengiyumva, primary school teacher:
Fighting against burnout and for social cohesion among colleagues

The PAP training inspired me to take better care of my colleagues and develop activities against the fatigue and burnout symptoms I sensed among the staff. We are about 25 teachers in our school. I founded a teacher's choir that regularly participates in events and has become very popular. I created a teachers' fund to which every teacher deposits a certain amount and it is used for mutual assistance when financial problems arise. Teachers can receive credits at a 3% interest rate. We also started a school hairdressers, with each teacher investing 5,000 Franc (about 6.50 €). This shop has so far made a profit of 100,000 Francs (130 €)! All these initiatives owe their creation to the PAP training. Without gaining the encouragement and empowerment we would have never found the self-esteem or strength to start such initiatives.

Josée Nyiramana, primary school teacher: How I dealt with my burnout

After finishing secondary school, I immediately started work as a 9th grade teacher. Then after a year I changed schools and later became the principal of a newly-established school centre. I was obliged to acquire the dignified behaviour traits and skills of a person in authority, such as concentration, tolerance, collaboration, and comprehension. I was given increasing responsibility and liked my job even more.

After getting married, I took up still more responsibilities, at school and at home, becoming a wife and mother as well as a teacher. I worked three times harder than before and had much less time to rest. I became nervous, fatigued, I couldn't sleep, got indigestion and many other sicknesses. To forget about my problems, I started drinking and smoking. As the symptoms worsened I consulted a doctor and took an 18-month break from work, ate healthily and made time for relaxation and exercise.

> After 18 months I went back to school and took part in the PAP training. When we came to the topic about burnout, I realized that I'd lived this very situation. I talked about my case and was given advice that I follow strictly. Currently my health situation is normal: I don't smoke; I can straighten out and braid my hair; I participate in all lively activities both inside and outside of school. Thanks to PAP, I have no more problems and feel very well.

Training structure

How should trainings in learner-centred education be organized to ensure that the content learned will be relevant to the teachers and can be implemented in their daily teaching practice?

(1) *Relation to Practice*:
- What's been learned must be experienced in the field: During training, teachers must be given the opportunity to directly apply the contents of the course. This can be best achieved by self-guided learning steps.
- Linking training topics to practice helps teachers easily implement them into daily school activities. This can be achieved by giving examples of application and reflecting upon them, or developing teaching activities while using newly acquired knowledge and skills.
- After the training, ongoing supervision and ongoing interactions between trainers and participants, as well as mutual exchanges between participants will ensure sustainability (see 2.2.3).

(2) *Relevance of teachers' personal and professional experiences:*
- The training should address the teachers' experiences and professional lives so as to enhance their self-reflection and personal growth.
- In post-conflict situations, it is crucial allow space and time for mourning, trauma work and healing. Likewise, teachers should be made aware of their students' issues which may be similar to their own, or even worse.

(3) *Relation between content and method:*
- Course content should be taught in a way that explains the primary importance of core social competencies. Teachers must reflect on their own convictions and learn to correlate theory and practice.

3 Implementing Social Competencies in Schools

- The content and methods used during training should correspond. It would be counterproductive to train teachers in the participatory and active approach using outdated methods. Teachers need hands-on experience of the methods as well as the techniques during their training. Experienced-based learning increases the probability of successful future implementation.
- The maxim "Do unto others as you would have them do unto you" can be applied to teachers when changed to, "Do unto the teachers as you would have them do unto students." Teachers often treat their students the same way they were treated as students. During their training, teachers must be able to experience the democratic, active and participatory approach in their relationships with the trainers.

(4) *Conditions that facilitate implementation:*
- At least two people from each school should attend a training course in order to be able to continue an exchange about their experiences after the course ends. The most effective training courses are those that include a school's entire teaching staff.
- Training should be planned over the long term to allow for systematic implementation. To identify and address the individual participant's attitudes and enable changes where necessary, each course unit should comprise at least ten days.
- Training course content should be communicated in advance to principals and administrators of participating schools. School officials should support and assist teachers in implementing the new insights they learned during the course (see 2.2.2).
- Training objectives must be clearly communicated throughout the school and associated community, including parents and parent associations, so everyone understands the importance and potential benefits (see 2.2.3).
- Appropriate incentives to undertake further education may be required. These might constitute increased prestige or a positive remark in a teacher's personnel file or portfolio. In regions where teachers' situations are precarious, cash payments or other incentives could be considered.

Experiences from PAP: The course of the training

The PAP program provides further training in learner-centred pedagogy for working teachers from all types of schools: nursery, primary and secondary. In addition to teacher training, a separate course in participative school management gives school administrators tools to promote the new PAP approach and also ways to improve and reinforce their management skills.

Training groups are formed according to the school type with at least 50% of the entire teaching staff of the same school participating; if possible the entire teaching staff should take part in the training. Places are reserved for one representative from the parents' council and one from the local government. Trainings are organized according to region to facilitate ongoing exchanges among participating teachers after the training and follow-up.

The program consists of four consecutive phases:

- A three-week basic training course in theories and concepts of learner-centred pedagogy held during the school holidays. It includes two weeks of coursework followed by a week of practical implementation and evaluation. The course combines active methods (group and partner work, interviews, role plays, etc.) together with units on learning theory and psychology. Communication theories and practical exercises (e.g. using I-messages) are integrated into the program.
- A pedagogical follow-up of supervision during two years,
- During the two years of follow-up and supervision lessons are visited by the training team on a regular base.
- Teachers are invited to submit lessons plans of lessons and discuss them together.

During the three-week basic training, participants live at a training centre and receive free food and accommodation. They receive a small stipend of US$15 to cover some basic necessities.

Conditions for success

Besides being well organized, a successful training course is one that gives space for participants to open up and change. It succeeds when teachers can implement what they've learned into their professional life. Therefore an open and pleasant atmosphere, established through an adequate location and friendly trainers, is important. The organizing structure of the teacher training needs to express appreciation towards the participants through good organization, punctual beginning, sufficient food, and an appealing ambiance. In post-conflict situations, the safety of the participants as well as their provision is of particular importance.

Objectives, content, and methods of the seminar have to be congruently coordinated. Training on social competencies and learner-centred education isn't convincing if organized as »chalk and talk«. Instead, the new approach needs be made attractive to teachers by already implementing it in the training. As mentioned before, changing attitudes needs time and a constant confrontation. Therefore it is important to have a phase after the basic training, where the implementation is being supported by supervision and collegial consultation (see chap. 3.3).

Experiences in PAP:
The relationship among content, structure and methods
The program focuses on the demand to place the child at the centre of the learning process. Therewith, the traditionally passive role of the student in class as well as the authoritarian basic structure in school should be overcome. The school should be developed regarding the learning success and as a basis for a democratic education. Therefore the training is organized according to the learner-centred approach in a way that participants are able to experience this pedagogical approach themselves, in the sense of "learning by doing" or rather "learning by experiencing". The training is non-specific in its domain, i.e. it addresses teachers of all subjects. The course combines activating didactic methods (group work, partner work, interviews, role plays, etc.) with units on learning theory and psychology, which refer to a constructivist understanding of learning and teaching. In addition, communication theories as well as practical exercises on communication (e.g. the sending of I-messages) are integrated into the program. After the two-week training, the participants practically apply what they've learned in a local school, and then jointly analyse it (one week).

Experiences from PAP: Successful organization of trainings
- Keep groups small (no more than 40 participants)
- Train teachers according to their school type; do not mix teachers from different school types
- Train all teachers from one school. This increases the likelihood of implementing the new approach in the school
- Involve the principals. It is a lot easier to implement a new approach if it is supported by the principal.

- Involve the parents/parent committee. Parents are often reserved when it comes to pedagogical innovation. Including them in the planning and/or training as well as the follow-up will enable them to understand the approach.
- Find a training location which houses all participants; it's important for the dynamics of the group and to build up trust within the group.
- Prepare the training well (administration, content, technology, and finances)
- Try to integrate the participants' expectations into the course and have them participate in the preparation.
- Agree on rules for the time of the training.
- Each day, evaluate what happened during the day and celebrate the completion of the seminar.
- Divide the country/province in clusters with regional coordinators.

Tips for running a seminar
Welcoming the participants

- Be present when the participants arrive
- Welcome participants and introduce yourself
- Prepare name tags or hand out badges so participants can write their own names
- Arrange an area for participants to congregate before the seminar starts

Starting the session

- Provide practical information regarding meals, breaks, use of cell phones and restrooms, external visitors, etc.

Providing information about training and objectives

- Summarize training objectives and program content
- Give overview that a learner-centred seminar requires personal involvement and learning activities.
- Encourage participants to interrupt, ask questions, express their fears, criticisms as well as what they hope to get out of the training experience.

Ending the seminar

- Collect all the texts for the documentation.
- Present information on the implementation and follow-up segments of the course.

- Introduce the supervisor for the follow-up section.
- Evaluate the seminar (see for example chap. 3.5).
- Invite local authorities to the official closing ceremony.
- Congratulate the participants for their successful participation in the seminar.
- Celebrate the successful completion of the seminar.
- Hand out participation certificates.

3.2 Involving the Stakeholders

A school comprises more than teachers and students. The entire teaching faculty plays an important role within the school, as does the administration, management, parents, and community. Changing the school requires a consensus from the majority of teachers, augmented by input from school officials and community members. Representatives of the national education system and regional ministers can also be included. It's advisable to involve the local stakeholders before the training starts.

The teaching staff

Changing teaching staff practices can be difficult. School administrators cannot leave innovating a school's learning culture to chance or to individual efforts by a few teachers. Instead, the entire school must systematically work towards the stated goal.

Cooperating as a team: Teachers work autonomously in class and are normally alone in the classroom. Generally, people cooperate as long as this doesn't interfere with their own areas of autonomy. To promote social competencies and learner-centred education means teachers must give up some autonomy in favour of successfully achieving mutually beneficial joint objectives. Open communication among all the stakeholders about the benefits of training inspires the staff to accept introducing new methods. Where such a culture isn't well-developed, it takes time for everyone to reorient their perceptions of their jobs and evolve into a "professional learning community" (Rolff, 2007).

Informing teachers: The teaching staff must be kept informed about the upcoming changes. An efficient course is based on the teachers' common understanding of the needs of the school. Before starting training, it is worth taking two hours to exchange with the teaching staff about the situation at school.

Adapting new ideas instead of just copying them: Disseminating a new idea involves the processes adaption and acquisition, not merely imposing or parroting an idea. Participating teachers learn to acquire new knowledge and techniques and adapt it to their particular classroom situations. Altrichter and Wiesinger (2005) refer to the advantages of an "evolutionary-adaptive approach of implementation" versus a "programmed approach", meaning that copying does often not work but contents of training have to be adapted to the personal reality. It may be useful to begin implementing the learner-centred education in a few classes with committed teachers and then expand it throughout the school. Increased mobility of teachers means schools that have already been fully trained can end up with new and untrained teachers. In this situation, their already trained colleagues can introduce them to practical aspects of the PAP methods through an "initiation" process. If required, a team of trainers is available to help mentor their trained colleagues. The so-called "assistant mentors" show the teacher how to act as a counsellor and guide for the new trainees, rather than judge their teaching skills.

Dealing with Resistance: Resistance is often an indication of problems. One way of handling the situation is to positively interpret the resistance and address it by discussing the benefits to be gained from the training. Start by working with the interested colleagues. Once the reticent teachers see the positive effects on their peers, they'll probably be excited to join too.

Including principals and administrators

Principals and administrators play key roles in any school. In many countries they hire teaching staff and direct teaching approaches. Trying to implement a new teaching approach against the will of a principal is counterproductive. Principals must be included in the process of introducing learner-centred education from its inception; they could also be invited to participate in the teacher training. Joint meetings of the administration and teaching staff help facilitate a climate in which innovations in the school culture and new approaches to teaching can be discussed.

3 Implementing Social Competencies in Schools

Participatory Management Program

During the Rwandan PAP program, special trainings were organized for school administrators and principals. Training upper level management avoids the potential problem of having trained teachers and their students dealing with a management still committed to the non-participatory approach. Additionally, the principals participated in the teacher training.

Participatory management training consists – as for the teachers – of three one-week modules. The first presents a general introduction to participatory management, addressing the main understanding and how to implement participatory management in schools. The second module covers time management, team-building, managing and motivating through projects, creativity and innovation as the core of participation, and communication for performance and participation. The third module deals with conflict and general management, the performance contract, methods of participatory management, how to start and manage a school project, evaluation and motivation of human resources, and practical advice on managing a school.

Parental resistance to new approaches

Parents often worry about their kid's academic achievement and can be reluctant to support new teaching policies, particularly because at first glance, the new methods of learner-centred education may appear more lax than the traditional ones. Some parents can't believe learning occur without corporal punishment. They're used to hearing teachers shouting at students and students shouting back. If school management meets with the parents' association or committees they can introduce the new approach and explain its expected implications. Similarly, such meetings provide parents with the opportunity to ask questions and express their concerns.

Adopting new democratic approaches also changes the relationships between students and teachers and the interactions of students and teachers among themselves. These changed relationships can ultimately influence the community at large. Parents must be informed and prepared for the possible outcomes related to implementing such a powerful new teaching approach.

Involving parents in PAP

In case of the PAP program in Rwanda, specific seminars or at least meetings are held to inform and sensitize the parents about the new approach about to be introduced in their school. They usually take place after the teacher training and before the implementation in school. Additionally, parents are associated to the follow-up in class after the training, so that they themselves can see and experience the changes in class.

Political stakeholders

In many countries including Rwanda, the educational system is governed by the state through its ministry of education. Any changes to the system usually require permission from the local authorities. To ensure the government understands and approves of the new PAP teaching system, it's important to educate governmental authorities, especially if more than one school is adopting the program. This becomes even more important in post-conflict situations where governments are re-establishing a sense of normalcy and new ideas might seem threatening.

Involving political stakeholders

In Rwanda, informational meetings at the ministerial level were held before the inception of the PAP program to involve the appropriate government officials. Once the program was up and running, ongoing three-day workshops were held for district education officers to keep them updated with the progress of the PAP implementation. Heads of different churches were often included in these workshops. Similarly, local authorities were always invited to contribute to or participate in the PAP trainings. They held workshops, introduced topics in the seminar, or joined in the inaugural or closing ceremonies of the seminar.

3.3 Follow-up and Supervision

Teacher's attitudes don't change after a single training but evolve and mature over time. Teachers need ongoing help in applying the new approaches in their daily classes.

Building a professionally run support structure

To supervise different schools within a region, a structure is needed that provides this specific region with professionals able to do the supervision and follow-up. They can be recruited from experienced teachers and then receive special training for this job. It would be helpful to have these people employed by the organization running the program. They could either be centrally located in the organization's main office, but could also be stationed in a more decentralized and regional way.

> **Experiences from PAP: Building a professional structure**
>
> The PAP training program in Rwanda has a two-pronged structure. A team of five in the capital city of Kigali oversees the entire PAP program, raises operating costs abroad, keeps the accounts, is part of the seminar training staff, and supervises other trainers. Each person is responsible for coordinating PAP activities in one province. In addition, twenty five regular working teachers have been trained in how to conduct PAP trainings. They work in teams of three and are paid for running trainings during school holidays. Thanks to this structure, several trainings can be held simultaneously, thus reaching more people at the same time.
>
> Between 2000 and 2012, a total of 2,500 teachers in more than 350 Rwandan schools received PAP training. The percentages include 32% of all protestant nursery schools, 37% of all protestant primary schools, and 27% of all protestant secondary schools. Based on the World Bank teacher-student ratio, more than 830,000 students have PAP-trained teachers.

Post training support

After-training support for teachers serves to reassure them that help is available should difficulties arise. Colleagues or training-staff members observe teachers' lessons and provide feedback on how they're implementing the learner-centred concepts. Constructive criticism enables teachers to improve their performance and stay motivated. Teachers need to know they aren't left on their own, but instead can discuss problems or questions that arise with the new approach.

Consulting with other colleagues provides another opportunity for teachers to share their problems and successes with the new approach. Peers play an important role as they work in the same environment and face similar challenges and problems. One teacher's solution might also work for others and save time by transferring best practice from one teacher to another. Additionally, collegial consultation improves the relations among colleagues and builds up trust in others and oneself.

Tips from practice: Collegial counselling

During collegial counselling, participants change the role from consulter to consultant. According to a defined scheme, the potential of the group is being used to assistingly reflect upon tasks, problems or conflicts and develop possible solutions. "Collegial" refers to the equal, collegial status of the members, not to a joint belonging to an organization. Due to a set course of the method, the opinion and advice of each member can be heard. This method benefits from the heterogeneity of a group.

Firstly it has to be decided who needs counselling and who takes over the role of the facilitator (keeping track of time, rules, and methodological steps).

The counselling itself has five phases:

(1) Presentation of the case by the consulter. The case is shortly explained.
(2) Inquiry by the consultants: Questions on understanding the situation, further information.
(3) Exchange between the consultants: Exchange on the respective views on the situation: ideas, hypotheses, fantasies.
(4) Proposal of solutions and action steps: Expressing concrete opportunities for action for the consulter.
(5) Statement of the consulter: announcing which idea and which advice has been attractive, where he or she wants to think further, but also what hasn't been helpful. (Cf. Antz et al. 2009, 93–94)

Follow-up and supervision in schools

During the follow-up in schools and the supervision of teachers, it is helpful to not only focus on the teaching alone, but also target the overall quality of the school which should be improved with the implementation of the new teaching approach.

To help teachers with the implementation of the new approach, lessons need to be observed. When observing lessons, it is important to have clear criteria on which the feedback is going to be based. The criteria need to be linked to the overall aims of the program and be operationalized into observable indicators. These indicators need to be prepared in advance and not randomly chosen by the observer. This allows comparison as the same indicators can be applied in different lessons of the same teacher to mark a development, but also in lessons of different teachers.

To supervise the overall development of the school, different aspects can be considered, that need to be linked to the training program as well. With a program based on social competences, a positive development of the school climate is expected. To supervise this aspect, questions about the well-being of students and teachers, the improvement of the situation of girls, or the cooperation among the teaching staff can be asked. Also, parents could be asked for feedback. In regard to raising the teaching quality (that should lead to a better student performance), statistics on drop-out rates, the passing of exams, or the transfer to the next level of schools (secondary school or university) could be observed.

Positive changes seen after implementing PAP

After PAP training, teachers use active methods in their lessons such as group work, short historical stories, structured exercises, brainstorming, etc. Desks are arranged in a semi-circle to enable better communication between teacher and students. Students and teachers exhibit completely changed behaviours; they work together in a positive atmosphere. The weak students participate actively in class and express their views freely without humiliation, especially during group work where they work with the strong students

The teachers testify that PAP helps them to successfully manage their overcrowded classes especially through group work. The conflicts or tensions which existed between teachers before their PAP-training are almost gone. They easily communicate with each other and show mutual support. The success rate in the exams has improved noticeably. In 6th grade for example, the success rate has grown from 62% in 2008 to 82.2% in 2009 and to 91.4% in 2010.

3.4 The Trainers

Finding and training trainers

The success of trainings in learner-centred education depends on the skills of the trainers. Trainers should have teaching experience incorporating the new approach and be accepted by the teacher trainees.

It isn't always easy to find people with the necessary qualifications, especially in post-conflict situations where the majority of people are dealing with trauma. Sometimes it is helpful to employ somebody with training experience from a different school maintaining body or from a different country to train the trainers. In this case, there needs to be a close cooperation between the organization running the program and the external trainer. The aims of the training, the methods, and the concept of the training need to be agreed upon. Then, a first training can be run and the implementation of the trained teachers in schools be supervised. During the supervision the best implementers become visible. These teachers can then receive an additional train-the-trainer training, including didactical aspects of adult education, and a theoretically profound consolidation of the training contents. This should equip the future trainers with the necessary knowledge and skills to run trainings on their own.

> **Experiences from PAP: Hiring trainers**
>
> Shortly after the end of the genocide, the decision was taken to run a teacher training program with a new approach. Since the necessary competences to run such a program were not available, a trainer was hired externally. In 1998, a Swiss teacher trainer arrived in Rwanda who developed the PAP training together with the local teacher training team. This teacher-trainer then initial a Rwandan team in their trainings and also helped train future trainers.

Working as a team

As one trainer cannot handle 40 people for three weeks there should be a group of three to four trainers. With a group of trainers, each brings a unique and specific set of competencies to the program. Just as teachers should not be left alone in the implementation of a new program, the trainers would also need space to share experiences, discuss problems, prepare trainings, and develop their skills and competences. Putting those trainers together in a group, they form a "professional learning community" (Stoll et al. 2006, 223), where they can together "seek and share learning". This increases their effectiveness as professionals.

The exact number and composition of trainers for each location can be decided on during a preparatory workshop that includes all the trainers. When choosing trainers to work in a team, it is important to consider different aspects in order to have a well-balanced and coherent team. Such a team needs people with profound theoretical and methodological knowledge, people who are able to flexibly adjust the planned program in case of need, and people who are able to socially animate the group (warm-ups, relaxation, spiritual needs, etc.). The team should be gender-balanced as it is sometimes easier to address topics or problems in gender homogeneous groups. Finally, it is important that the trainers get al.ong well, as personal animosities may overshadow and thus influence the training negatively.

As the team is working in a cooperative way, the responsibilities and tasks are shared among the group. The roles and responsibilities of the team members therefore need to be clearly defined. Content-wise, the topics are shared among the trainers which they prepare alone or in teams of two. Besides running the training content wise, there are a number of other aspects that need to be taken care of, such as the contact with headquarters or the press, the production of the documentary report, the evaluation of the training, or the working atmosphere. Those tasks can be spread among the members of the team but it needs to be clear who's in charge of what. It may also be helpful to have one team member function as a liaison between the participants and the team in case problems arise. There should be one person named the overall coordinator who is the last decision taker.

In post-conflict settings, the open nature of the trainings in learner-centred education can sometimes rekindle traumatic personal experiences or flashbacks. At least one team member should be trained in counselling and first-aid in trauma work to handle these potentially sensitive situations. It helps to have a database of psychological professionals trained in this work so participants could be transferred if a need arises.

> **Experiences from PAP: Cooperation between trainers and participants**
> For the time of the three-week training, the following roles and tasks were elected:
> - a formal representative in the training team of the seminars,
> - people or small groups in charge of the social life during the seminar (head of the village, time keeper, team of social affairs, team of morning bible meditation, team of information, etc.).

3.5 Quality Management

Quality management is crucial to ensuring a high-quality training program and is often required by external sponsors. It can take place at different levels looking at various aspects and involving different groups of people.

An adequate reporting system is vital and must include activities, participants, participant days, and supervision. These reports much be continued throughout the years of funding which can be a complex task, especially when many activities are decentralized. Therewith, data can be collected that may help to adjust the program in term of organizational efficacy.

> **Anathalie Munganyinka, primary school teacher: Better exam results**
> Before receiving PAP training, primary school teachers explained the subject using the traditional methodology and tests results were very low: Only 2.9% of the students passed the national exam in 2007.
> After the PAP-training, the active participation of the students and the regular follow-ups by the teacher/facilitator yielded remarkably positive results. Students helped each other; they demonstrated solidarity, creativity, innovation, and progress in understanding the subject. As a consequence of these positive changes, the test results steadily improved from one year to the next: 2.9% in 2007; 45.9% in 2008; 64.5% in 2009; 77.7% in 2010.
> Other grades also improved. In 2011, we held secondary classes for the first time. We realized that students coming from our school performed better than students coming from other schools. Our students prove they know the subject matter by explaining it to each other.

Innocent Gasana, secondary school teacher: Improving academic achievement

Before the PAP training I considered the students as unknowing. I spoke most of the time and the students never participated in the lessons.

The students performed well because all they had to do was reproduce the elements I gave them in the notes. However they failed the national exams because the questions addressed a general knowledge and creativity they didn't possess.

After the PAP training I changed my old teaching methods and gave the students time for discussion during the lessons. I also changed my way of asking them questions, adapting it to the types of questions asked in the state exam. These changes lead to the following results:

In 2006 before the PAP training, eight students out of 55 failed the national exam and five received university scholarships from the government. After the formation in 2007, five students out of 60 failed and six got university scholarships. In 2008, only three out of 68 failed the national exam, while 15 received university scholarships.

In order to ensure the content quality and the conduction of the program, it is important to do regular internal evaluations involving everybody responsible in the program. Therewith, experiences can be gathered and necessary readjustments in light of current developments can be carried out.

When being financed externally, it is appropriate to have external evaluations from time to time. No matter whether evaluations are internal or external, it is important to agree upon indicators. In case of external evaluations, clear terms should be fixed ahead. The goal of teacher training programs is to improve the students' social and educational performance. Therefore, regular monitoring of students' performance is paramount. The achievement ratio in national exams, transfer rate to secondary schools, or a decreased drop-out rates are all good performance indicators. These numbers should be gathered gender-sensitively and data should be assessed both for individual schools as well as pooled.

Experiences from PAP: Evaluating the PAP training

Towards the end of the training, participants receive a questionnaire related to objectives, content, methodology, trainers, setting, learning, and transfer. Answers are rated on a scale of 1 (excellent) to 6 (poor). Then, participants state whether they would participate in a similar training in the future (yes, no, uncertain).

They rate the usefulness of the program (very useful, useful, not useful). With a final question the trainer(s)' competences and methods are assessed. The floor then opens for further comments and suggestions.

3.6 Financial and Funding Requirements

Running a teacher training program on learner-centred education in a post-conflict situation requires a solid financial base and is an impossible undertaking without external funding. Considering the manifold problems countries face after civil wars or violent conflicts, investing in teacher training may not be a top priority. Yet money spent for such a program represents an important and necessary investment. Schools play a crucial role in re-establishing normalcy for conflict-affected children and youth. Additionally, quality education is an important component for the future of every society.

Long-term funding

Teacher-training programs that aim to change attitudes and behaviours cannot succeed overnight. It takes significant time and effort to train teacher-trainers and teachers in learner-centred approaches. Looking at a whole country, it requires years until enough teachers have been trained before a paradigm shift occurs within the education system. Therefore, teacher training programs need to be long-term programs and as such, a long-term financial funding is necessary. A five year period of funding – the regular funding period in development programs – will not lead to sufficient outcome.

> **Experiences from PAP: Long-term funding in different phases**
>
> This program has been funded for over 15 years. However, and this seems to be of relevance for such a program, the long-term perspective of the financial support wasn't part of the project contract in the first place. Instead, the project was based on a long-term partnership option with several different phases running between three to five years, each phase having its own special focus. While training teachers was always the main priority of the PAP program in Rwanda, within each funding cycle, different priorities were assigned to the different phases of the program.

Immediately after the genocide, teachers needed training in trauma work and counselling. During the second phase of funding the program the focus shifted to increasing the number of PAP programs within the primary school sector. This increased the demand for qualified teacher-trainers for the primary sector and led more trainings and higher participant rates. During the third phase of funding the increasing number of trainings within the primary school sector was maintained. In addition, new target groups (secondary schools, early childhood education, nursery schools) were added, along with training for the school management and administration.

Types of costs

Teacher training programs in post-conflict countries incur a variety of expenses that must be included in the overall budget

- *Salaries:* Salaries are needed for the program manager and other employees, including the accountant.
- *Fees:* Trainer fees are required. Local teachers who become trainers and who lead trainings occasionally while working their regular teaching jobs also requires payment.
- *Training costs*: A budget for accommodation, food, travel and materials is required for the participants of every training program.

Experiences from PAP: Which contribution can be expected of teachers?
During the discussion phase of the teacher training program, the standard of accommodation was considered and teachers were questioned as to how much they could contribute to the costs. In order to save money on accommodation, the participants were asked to bring along a blanket to be accommodated in a school where also the food should be cooked – as trainings take place during the holidays, this did not pose a problem. This idea turned out to be impractical as most teachers only owned one blanket and this would have left the spouse without it. Training the teachers during the day and then letting them leave for the night was not an option as it would not strengthen the social cohesion among the participants. Additionally, the team was afraid that the participants would not be able to focus on the training. The various options considered turned out to be less practical than using simple and cheap conference centres.

Since accommodation, food and transport were covered, participants didn't require a per diem allowance. However they were allocated a small sum for incidentals and to partially cover the three weeks of salary they wouldn't be earning during the training period. Each teacher received 10,000 Rwandan Francs (~ 15.00 €).

- *Costs for meetings and preparatory workshops:* To ensure continued high-quality trainings, the teacher trainers need to get together for pre-session preparation and post-session evaluations. Transportation, food and accommodation (if required) for these meetings must be covered.
- *Public relations and related material:* Well-run public relations campaigns ensure a broad acceptance of the training program by professionals and the public. Meetings with school inspectors at different levels and visits to ministries and school authorities are important components of public information. Communicating with those in charge of private schools is also important. Time, transportation and accommodation (if necessary) also require funding. A budget must be created for producing flyers and publishing handbooks or other training materials. Lectures, round tables, and short "demonstration" trainings also require funding.
- *Office equipment:* The office requires modern computers, telephone and internet access, and a sturdy photocopier to reproduce the necessary training materials. Those using the computers will require training and a technical support service. Funds for electricity, water, a generator and surge protectors must be budgeted for.
- *Training equipment:* A well-run training needs adequate sufficient equipment. For example, running five training sessions simultaneously would require five overhead projectors, five portable photocopiers, a digital camera for each training location (to document the results) plus flipcharts, paper, and posters.
- *Transport/off-road vehicles:* Access to schools located in rural areas can be difficult. To work effectively, the training team needs an off-road vehicle and driver.
- *Evaluations:* Evaluations should be financed at regular intervals, as they give important stimulus for the further development of the program (see chap. 4). The financial framework of the evaluation should be adequate to the specific program.

Experiences from PAP: Financial need

Between its inception in 1997 and 2012, a total of 3,900.000 € was spent on the entire PAP program in Rwanda. Since 2000, more than 2,500 teachers and principals have been trained in PAP at an individual training cost of 1,560 € per person. Approximately 830,000 students have benefitted from the program which translates to a training cost of about 4.70 € per student. (This calculation is based on the World Bank's teacher-student-ratio.)

Running a PAP teacher training program in a post-conflict situation like Rwanda requires a solid financial base and is an impossible undertaking without external funding. Considering the manifold problems countries face after civil wars or violent conflicts, investing in teacher training may not be a top priority. Yet money spent for such a program represents an important and necessary investment. Schools play a crucial role in reestablishing normalcy for conflict-affected children and youth. Additionally, quality education is an important component for the future of every society. Therefore the funding for such important work is well invested money.

4 Does it Work? Results from Research

This chapter presents the results of our impact evaluation of the "Participatory and Active Pedagogy" program in Rwanda. The positive effects of the program documented herein provide incentives to institute other similar programs in post-conflict-regions.

4.1 Empiric Analysis of Learner-Centered Education

As explained in Chapter 2 and 3, core social competencies and learner-centered education make an important contribution to the quality of teaching and education. But can a three-week teacher training change teachers' attitudes and behavior enough to manifest as socially competent behavior on the part of their students? Does PAP really contribute to a more peaceful class climate? Does it affect the students' and teachers' self-concepts?

> **PAP program evaluations**
>
> The PAP program was evaluated three times by external bodies. In 2000, the German Federal Ministry for Economic Cooperation and Development recommended continuing the project and suggested several minor administrative improvements (cf. Cécé et al. 2001). In 2005, the program an international team led by Michel Moukouri-Edeme focused on the program and its possible continuation (cf. Broutier et al. 2005). The team recommended expanding the program from only primary schools to also include secondary schools. In 2010, a team from a German university, led by Annette Scheunpflug, conducted an outcome evaluation. They described the positive impacts of the program on teachers as well as students and noted aspects that could be developed further (cf. Krogull & Scheunpflug 2010). The results of this evaluation are presented in this chapter.

> **Agnès Nyirangirimana, teacher in Nyarusange:**
> **Homage to the Participatory and Active Pedagogy**
> An important initial sign of the success of the PAP training was the positive feedback received from many participants, some of whom expressed their feelings in poetry.

4 Does it Work? Results from Research

Training in PAP [shortened]

Inexhaustible source
Unbelievable force
Impeccable tool
Invisible letter
O active pedagogy!

At your bottom swells the energy
Your eyes towards the horizon
With popular topics
Founder of loyalty
You develop the activity
And accentuate effectiveness.
You become a canal
Leading to the womb
Gaining trust

You cause true judgment
By calming the feelings
You caress the brain

Your active methods
With a creative word
The children become analysts
With gestures and words
They confront problems.

Your impressive methods
Under the patronage of the instructions
You hate indifference.

Athalie Nyiranzigiyimana and Jean Baptiste Ndigendereho, trained in Rutsiro district: The Time Arrives [shortened]

We were very far,
We were lost
We did what isn't good without knowledge
Then the CPR arrives
In our district of Rutsiro
To give us knowledge

Unbelievable but true
Untraceable but seen
Impossible but done
Uncorrectable but corrected
Have you guessed this
It's the use of the ancient method
Method of exposition
Method that blocks the students' research
Method that provokes shyness
Method that ignores the student
Even though it is him who is the center of learning

Dear colleagues help me that we all say
Good-bye to the expository method
In these three weeks
We have learnt many things.
Do you remember the useful tools
To apply this pedagogy?
Such as the dictation in class
Brainstorming
Working in groups
I-message and others.

It a good method
Method that supports the students' development
Method that supports the spirit of creativity
Method that develops the sense of responsibility.

With this pedagogy, we will give quality
With it, we will consider our students
With it, we will support the habit of success
With it, we will be loved by our students
With it, we will change the world.

Objective of an evaluation

An evaluation that looks at whether and how many objectives are achieved must assess results from both the teachers' and students' points of view. Much can be achieved if teachers change, but what about the students? Do they display greater self-esteem and less fear? What do they think about the teachers, the teaching and themselves as students in a class? How do they assess their relationships with the teacher and those with their fellow students? Which professional conceptions do teachers have about their role and how do they describe these?

PAP impact evaluation: Method

We developed a control group design since a pre-post comparison was not possible and the many different variables made a longitudinal study equally impossible. "PAP schools" (schools with teachers who had participated in the training) were compared to "non-PAP schools" (control schools) where the teachers had not yet received the PAP training. For purposes of comparison, the non-PAP control schools were chosen based on features similar to those of the PAP schools. All were low-fee private schools run by various Protestant churches. Comparative criteria included: school location of (rural or urban); school fees; parents' professional backgrounds of the parents (agricultural, commercial etc.); condition of the school buildings and infrastructure.

Recent research on schools and classroom indicates that the impact of school education depends on a number of interrelated factors (cf. esp. Helmke 2010). Based on this research and the aims of the program as reflected in the discussions with the team running the program, we developed an impact model, which is shown in fig. 3). To control these aspects, we also included data from the school as well as the family background of the participants (teachers and students).

4 Does it Work? Results from Research

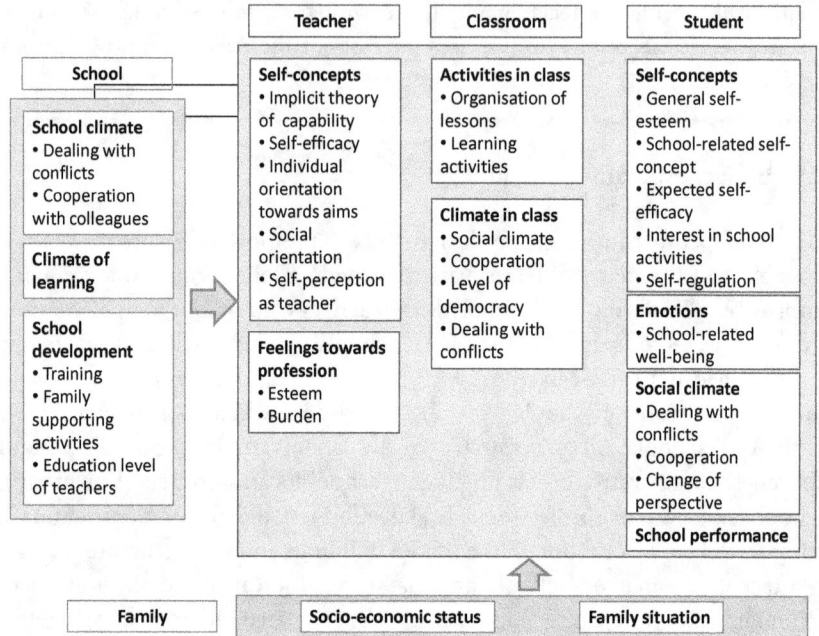

Fig. 3: *Model of the interrelationships between various study aspects. Adapted from Haertel, Walberg & Weinstein 1983/1993, Helmke & Weinert 1997.*

The instruments

The data was collected using questionnaires (cf. Krogull & Scheunpflug 2010) and realigned with data from class observation. Questionnaires consisted of proven and tested item batteries from international and German studies such as: PISA 2000 and 2006; PIRLS 2001 a study on democracy (Diedrich et al. 2004); two studies on students' and teachers' traits (Schwarzer & Jerusalem 1999; Gerecht et al. 2007); a Swiss-German study on teaching quality (Klieme et al. 2005); a German one on the same topic (Ditton & Merz 2000); a study on self-esteem (Collani & Herzberg 2003); two studies on motivation (Ziegler et al. 2005; Dresel 2008).

Background of the measurement is the operationalization of core social competencies in psychological constructs as self-concept and self-efficacy. The concept of self-efficacy is based on Bandura (1977), who distinguishes between a person's expected result and expected efficacy. While the expected result specifies which behavior leads to success or failure, the expected efficacy addresses the question whether one considers oneself capable of executing a certain behavior leading to success. Moschner & Dickhäuser (2006) describe self-efficacy as "a person's conviction to be able to successfully execute a behavior which is necessary to reach a certain result of action" (629). Key resources for self-efficacy are coping experiences (success vs. failure), substitutional experiences in which self-efficacy is being fed by the observation of a successful or unsuccessful model, feedback from a third person and physiological and affective conditions in which people suggest a lack of competence due to their strong agitation in a situation of performance (cf. Jonas & Brömer 2002). Cooperation is operationalized following Eder (2006; 627), who describes the interaction of favorable effects in which an orientation towards cooperation is involved as follows: Where "an individualizing and supporting teacher-student-interaction, especially solicitousness, student-centered attitude, and an (individual) reference norm orientation appear in connection with a cooperative and emotionally positive student-student-interaction [...], a strong enhancement especially of the school self-efficacy can be detected. Those influence significantly the school performance, the feeling in school and test anxiety". Rost and Schermer (2006) also report that strengthening the in-class cooperation prevents performance anxiety among students.

So far, data on forms of social learning have only been collected in industrialized countries. Given the language capabilities in Rwanda, it was clear that this study needed to be undertaken in Kinyarwanda and that questionnaires would need to be translated. They underwent a double translation between German and Kinyarwanda (translation and re-translation) plus multiple discussions with Rwandese linguistic and education experts. After a pre-test that comprised 405 students, 37 teachers and 2 principals, the questionnaires were reworked again with a double translation and expert discussion before reaching their final state.

Nevertheless, the internal consistency of the scales did not reach the same value as in the original international or European studies. This could be due to the large heterogeneity in Rwandan classes in terms of educational level, age and personal experiences. Applying factor analysis and excluding items often did not help improve the internal consistency (measured by Cronbach's alpha). The data shows a tendency towards undifferentiated ratings (i.e. most ratings are at one or the other end of the scales). Student grades in Kinyarwanda ability were checked to eliminate the possibility that the poor Cronbach's alphas are due to lack of reading capability, or the wide range of the age groups within the classes. The aspects covered by the teacher and student questionnaires are presented in tables 2 and 3.

Table 2: Examples from the teacher questionnaire

Aspects	Example item
General self-efficacy (Schwarzer & Jerusalem 1999) (10 items)	"I can find a solution for any problem." (1 to 4 rating scale: 1 = I disagree, 4 = I agree a lot)
Teaching self-efficacy (Schwarzer & Jerusalem 1999) (9 items)	"I know I can manage to teach everything relevant for the test, even to the most problematic students." (1 to 4 rating scale: 1 = I disagree, 4 = I agree a lot)
The implicit theory of capability (Ziegler et al. 2005) (9 items)	"My students cannot really change anything about how talented they are." (1 to 6 rating scale: 1 = I disagree a lot, 6 = I agree a lot)
Orientations towards competition (Dresel 2008) (5 items)	"In my lessons I attach great importance to motivating students through competition." (1 to 6 rating scale: 1 = I disagree a lot, 6 = I agree a lot)
Orientation towards cooperation and Individual learning (Dresel 2008) (10 items)	"In my lessons I attach great importance to letting students help each other." (1 to 6 rating scale: 1 = I disagree a lot, 6 = I agree a lot)
Social orientation (Gerecht et al. 2007) (4 items)	"I take time during class for personal and social matters." (4 to 6 rating scale: 1 = I disagree a lot , 4 = I agree a lot)
Esteem (PISA 2000) (3 items)	"Do you think society appreciates your work?" dichotomous rating scale, 0 = no, 1 = yes).
Burden (Schwarzer & Jerusalem 1999) (7 items)	"I often feel overwhelmed." (1 to 5 rating scale: 1 = I disagree a lot , 5 = I agree a lot)
Learner-centered learning activities (PISA 2000) (10 items)	"In my lessons students work in small groups." (1 to 6 rating scale: 1 = never, 6 = in almost every lesson)
Traditional learning activities (PISA 2000) (6 items)	"In my lessons students often speak in unison." (1 to 6 rating scale: 1 = never, = in almost every lesson)

Table 2: (continued)

Aspects	Example item
Democratic climate in class (Diedrich et al. 2004) (7 items)	"In my lessons I present different views on the same subject matter." (1 to 4 rating scale: 1 = never, 4 = often)
Students' level of democracy (Diedrich et al. 2004) (8 items)	"Our students can give reasons for their opinions." (1 to 4 rating scale: 1 = I disagree, 4 = I agree)
Violence by teachers (Diedrich et al. 2004) (8 items)	"A teacher hit a student." (1 to 4 rating scale: 1 = never, 4 = often)
School objectives (Klieme et al. 2005) (12 items)	"At my school we encourage the students' self-confidence." (1 to 6 rating scale: 1 = I disagree a lot, 6 = I agree a lot)

Table 3: Examples from the student questionnaire

Aspects	Example item
School self-efficacy (Schwarzer & Jerusalem 1999) (6 items)	"I can solve even difficult exercises in class if I make an effort." (1 to 4 rating scale: 1 = I disagree, 4 = I agree a lot)
Expected self-efficacy concerning social demands (Schwarzer & Jerusalem 1999) (8 items)	"I dare to say what I think even when others have different opinions." (1 to 4 rating scale: 1 = I disagree, 4 = I agree a lot)
Dealing with failure (Dresel 2008) (14 items)	"If I make a mistake, I enjoy class less than before." (1 to six rating scale: 1 = I disagree a lot, 6 = I agree a lot)
Self-esteem (Collani & Herzberg 2003) (8 items)	"I consider myself a valuable person, at least I'm no less valuable than other people." (1 to 4 rating scale: 1 = I disagree, 4 = I agree)
Self-regulation (Schwarzer & Jerusalem 1999) (10 items)	"After a break I can easily continue working." (1 to 4 rating scale: 1 = I disagree, 4 = I agree a lot)
General school self-concept (PISA 2000) (3 items)	"In most subjects I learn fast." (fo1 to 4 rating scale: 1 = I disagree, 4 = I agree)

Table 3: (continued)

Aspects	Example item
Subject specific self-concept (PISA 2000) (6 items)	"I get good grades in Kinyarwanda." (1 to 4 rating scale: 1 = I disagree, 4 = I agree)
Fear in class (Ditton & Merz 2000) (3 items)	"I'm afraid to raise my hand during class." (1 to 4 rating scale: 1 = I disagree a lot, 4 = I agree a lot)
Orientation towards cooperation (PISA 2000) (5 items)	"I learn most when working together with other students." (1 to 4 rating scale: 1 = I disagree, 4 = I agree)
Orientation towards competition (PISA 2000) (4 items)	"I like to try to be better than the other students." (1 to 4 rating scale: 1 = I disagree, 4 = I agree)
Adopting different perspectives (PISA 2000) (5 items)	"Before criticizing people I try to imagine how I would feel in their place." (1 to 4 rating scale: 1 = I disagree a lot; 4 = I agree a lot)
Structure of the lesson (Gerecht et al. 2007) (9 items)	"During the lesson the t content is often summarized." (1 to 4 rating scale: 1 = I disagree a lot, 4 = I agree a lot)
Learner-centered learning activities (PISA 2000) (7 items)	"We work in small groups." (1 to 4 rating scale: 1 = never, 4 = in all or half the lessons)
Traditional learning activities (PISA 2000) (6 items)	"In my lessons I talk and ask questions and single students reply." (1 to 4 rating scale: 1 = never, 4 = in all or half the lessons)
Students' teacher perception (PISA 2000) (5 items)	"Most of my teachers are interested in what I have to say." (1 to 4 rating scale: 1 = I disagree a lot; 4 = I agree a lot)
Student-teacher-relation (PISA 2000) (6 items)	"Our teachers have sympathy for our personal problems." (1 to 5 rating scale: 1 = I disagree a lot; 5 = I agree a lot)

Table 3: (continued)

Aspects	Example item
General school satisfaction (PISA 2000) (2 items)	"In my school I feel I am in good hands." (1 to 5 rating scale: 1 = I disagree a lot; 5 = I agree a lot)
Level of democracy (Diedrich et al. 2004) (10 items)	"My school is a place where I learn to give reasons for my opinions." (1 to 4 rating scale: 1 = I don't agree, 4 = I agree)
Violence by teachers (adapted from: Diedrich et al. 2004) (5 items)	"A teacher hit you." (1 to 4 rating scale: 1 = never, 4 = often)
Students as victims (adapted from: Diedrich et al. 2004) (9 items)	"A fellow student took something away from you against your will." (1 to 4 rating scale: 1 = never, 4 = often)
Students as perpetrators (adapted from: Diedrich et al. 2004) (9 items)	"You deliberately broke something in school." (1 to 4 rating scale: 1 = never, 4 = often)
Dealing with conflicts (Klieme et al. 2005) (8 items)	"If there are different opinions in class concerning an important question, we better not speak about it." (1 to 4 rating scale: 1 = I disagree a lot, 4 = I agree a lot)

The questionnaires and thus the results were made anonymous according to high scientific standards so that no relation could be established between the answers and the single participant.

International research has shown that the effects of teacher training on the attitudes of students are rather small. In so-called industrialized countries, and especially in the area of social learning, the effects of social learning are indicated to be small, as schools find themselves in competition with a variety of educational and socialization players who reduce the school's effects (cf. Scheerens & Bosker 1997; Baumert & Köller 1998). Therefore, large effects should not be expected. An evaluation of a multiannual project on democratic education in Germany showed that a significant and relevant increase for example in self-esteem or in adopting a different perspective could not be observed (cf. Abs et al. 2007; 58 f.). Despite their great efforts in the area of social learning, protestant schools in Germany reach only slightly higher results in the field of social cooperation than public schools (cf. Standfest, Köller & Scheunpflug 2005). Seeing the great importance of family education, especially in conveying values, even small results attributed to the program are important results. Based on these experiences of international research on the effects of teacher training statistically significant results of the PAP evaluation were expected to be rather small if existing at all.

Sample

A total of 976 students and 116 teachers participated in the survey. 549 students and 68 teachers came from PAP schools, 427 students and 48 teachers from non-PAP schools. The PAP schools and the non-PAP schools had been comparable in regard to socio-economic background, standards of life and general teacher qualification. The questionnaires and thus the results were made anonymous according to high scientific standards so that no relation could be established between the answers and the single participant. The National Institute of Statistics in Rwanda was informed about the study.

4.2 Findings 1: Improvement of Activation in Class

The following tables show the areas in which PAP schools demonstrate better results than non-PAP schools and where these differences are significant.. Aspects not displayed in the table also show a positive tendency in favor of PAP schools, but the difference didn't become significant.

Table 4: Comparison of teachers' perceptions

	PAP schools	Non-PAP schools
Preference for traditional learning activities ***	4.4 (SD 1.3)	5.3 (SD 0.9)
Preference for student-centered learning activities *	4.7 (SD 0.7)	4.3 (SD 0.9)
Communication between teachers ***	4.6 (SD 1.7)	1.1 (SD 1.6)

Note: *** = The difference between PAP schools and non-PAP schools is statistically highly significant ($p<.001$, i.e. the probability that the differences are not coincidental is higher than 99.9%)
* = the difference between PAP schools and non-PAP schools is statistically significant ($p<.05$, i.e. the probability that the differences are not coincidental is higher than 95%).
SD (standard deviation) describes how much variation exists from the average.

4 Does it Work? Results from Research

A crucial aspect of any training is whether or not the participants will implement the knowledge gained after the training. In case of the PAP training in Rwanda, teachers in PAP schools show a higher preference towards student-centered learning activities (working independently, debating, etc.) than teachers in non-PAP schools. They also show decreased preference for traditional learning activities (choral repetition, rote learning, etc.) than non-PAP teachers. Additionally, PAP training fosters the communication between teachers which leads to an increased professionalism as teachers exchange experiences, share ideas and discuss professional problems.

The students' answers about life at school validate the teachers' self-reported comments.

Table 5: Comparison of students' perceptions

	PAP schools	Non-PAP schools
New learning activities ***	3.00 (SD 0.6)	2.77 (SD 0,6)
Structured lesson **	3.61 (SD 0.4)	3.51 (SD 0.5)
Climate: Teacher *	3.42 (SD 0.6)	3.34 (SD 0.6)
Climate: School *	4.55 (SD 0.7)	4.42 (SD 0.9)
Fear in class **	1.79 (SD 0.9)	1.95 (SD 0.9)

Note: *** = The difference between PAP schools and non-PAP schools is statistically highly significant ($p<.001$, i.e. the probability that the differences are not coincidental is higher than 99.9%)
** = the difference between PAP schools and non-PAP schools is statistically significant ($p<.01$, i.e. the probability that the differences are not coincidental is higher than 99%);
* = the difference between PAP schools and non-PAP schools is statistically significant ($p<.05$, i.e. the probability that the differences are not coincidental is higher than 95%).

A key aspect of the students' perception of class is whether they understand the lesson structure and can follow actively in class. A clearly structured lesson encourages student participation. The atmosphere in the classroom is a key element of the learning environment. Implementing fosters a positive climate in class as well as in the whole school.

Results of the classroom observation validate these findings. PAP classes provided more opportunities for learner-centered participation than non-PAP classes (3.05 vs. 2.25). Additionally, the atmosphere in PAP classes was friendlier and more student-oriented (3.18 vs. 2.42).

4.3 Findings 2: Encouragement of Students' Personal Development

As described above, the students' self-esteem and self-efficacy was measured. When using a learner-centered methodology, students work self-dependently on exercises, and with the help of their obtained performance results and a corresponding feedback from the teacher experience themselves as the cause for their success. Parallel to the more positive school-related expected self-efficacy among PAP students, they also show a more positive self-esteem (see table 6 below). As before, aspects not displayed in the table also show a positive tendency in favor of PAP-schools, but the difference didn't become significant.

Table 6: Comparing students' perceptions

	PAP schools	Non-PAP schools
School-related expected self-efficacy**	3.28 (SD 0.5)	3.19 (SD 0.6)
Self-esteem *	3.28 (SD 0.7)	3.19 (SD 0.6)

Note: ** = the difference between PAP schools and non-PAP schools is statistically significant (p<.01, i.e. the probability that the differences are not coincidental is higher than 99%);
* = the difference between PAP schools and non-PAP schools is statistically significant (p<.05, i.e. the probability that the differences are not coincidental is higher than 95%).

Students in PAP schools show a higher school-related expected self-efficacy and have a higher self-esteem. Learner-centered pedagogy contributes to positive personal development.

4.4 Findings 3: Enhancement of Competences for Democracy and Peace

A spirit of cooperation is crucial to peaceful social interactions. We looked on cooperation among teachers. Here the orientation towards competition which is also significantly less among PAP teachers than non-PAP teachers (see table 7).

Table 7: Comparison of teachers' perceptions

	PAP schools	Non-PAP schools
Teacher orientation towards competition in class *	4.6 (SD 0.8)	5.0 (SD 0.8)

Note: * = the difference between PAP schools and non-PAP schools is statistically significant (p<.05, i.e. the probability that the differences are not coincidental is higher than 95%).

Accordingly, students in PAP schools rated the climate in school more positively than those in non-PAP schools. There are three statistically significant aspects which influence the positive climate in school: Students in PAP schools experience significantly more often a constructive dealing with conflicts as well as forms of school democratization while at the same time they are less often the target of violence by teachers.

The following table shows the areas in which PAP schools show not only better results than non-PAP schools, but where these differences are significant, which means that they are not coincidental, but structurally implied. Aspects not displayed in the table also show a positive tendency in favor of PAP schools, but the difference didn't become significant (see table 8).

Table 8: Comparison of students' perceptions

	PAP schools	Non-PAP schools
School's level of democracy***	3.18 (SD 0.4)	3.08 (SD 0.5)
Positive coping with conflicts***	2.65 (SD 0.6)	2.49 (SD 0.6)
Violence by teachers ***	1.87 (SD 0.8)	2.06 (SD 0.8)

Note: *** = The difference between PAP schools and non-PAP schools is statistically highly significant (p<.001, i.e. the probability that the differences are not coincidental is higher than 99.9%)

How conflicts are dealt contributes to a democratic climate. In PAP schools, conflicts in class are addressed and different opinions acknowledged. Instead of a few students doing all the talking, all the students are encouraged to discuss the conflict objectively and reach an agreement.

In PAP schools, students learn to justify their decisions and treat others the same way they themselves would like to be treated. Decisions by different actors in school are transparent and therefor understandable by the students. All this leads to a more democratic climate in school.

Whether students feel safe at and positive about school doesn't only depend on their academic achievement or opportunities for participation. They cannot learn well if they are subjected to violence, either by their teachers or by their fellow students. (The study also included questions on students as perpetrator of violence against fellow students). In schools where the program for learner-centered, participatory and active pedagogy is implemented, students experience less violence by their teachers than in non-PAP schools.

These results in all three aspects of this questionnaire show high significance emphasizes the relevance of learner-centered education. The results of class observation also support these findings. A democratic style of teaching and relating to one another was more common in PAP schools than in non-PAP schools (2.21 vs. 1.48). In this sense, this program of l leads to higher democratic competencies for peace because conflicts are addressed in positive and constructive ways and less violence occurs in schools.

Epilogue – Cooperation in a Global Context

This study is important not solely because of its results, but also for the process that lead to them. Evaluating peace education requires mutual trust and cooperation. The conditions of the study presented herein provide guidelines relevant to future cooperative research partnerships in this field of study.

We – the two German researchers and the local Rwandan teacher training team – could not have worked together for two years, nor could this book have been written, without the confluence of various factors (see for an overview about challenges in North-South research cooperation Lang-Wojtasik 2002; Ashcroft & Raynor 2011).

First, the responsibility for instituting the evaluation wasn't with the international donor or the international research team, but rather with the local teacher training team that spearheads the PAP program. They agreed to be evaluated, sought the funding, searched among various international candidates and chose us from among various international applicants.

As researchers we made great efforts to include the teacher training team at crucial points during the evaluation (see Joint Committee 2003; UNEG 2005). Data collection methods used in the schools were approved by the government school supervision. We provided personal feedback to the teachers whose lessons we observed, as well as to the school administrations of the participating schools. Possible consequences of our evaluation were discussed jointly. Wherever possible we presented results together with the team at meetings and conferences. The Rwandan team was familiar with evaluations and knew the process could help them develop their own work. Because the evaluation was linked to their positive expectation of qualified feedback, we didn't have to overcome any resistance.

To ensure local schools would accept being evaluated and to lend credence to our German research team, our Rwandan partners engaged a "consultative council." It supervised the design of the evaluation as well as the discussion and publication of results. Council members came from member churches, the ministry of education, a university and a private education provider. This lead to a triangle which was able to control the researchers' sovereignty of definition on the one hand, while on the other hand it lead to a larger public recognition of the results within the Rwandan public.

Another important factor for creating trust and cooperation was *being sensitive to issues of language*. All internal communication took place in French, a lingua franca that wasn't the mother tongue of any of the participants but that everybody was able to speak and write. After joining the Commonwealth in 2009, English became official language in Rwanda and language of instruction. Thus, our Rwandan partners requested that English be used at official meetings and that publications be in English.

One downside of everyone speaking a non-native language was the potential for missing the finer nuances of content. We tried to minimize this problem by patiently translating back and forth between the various languages. Evaluation results were presented in French as well in English. However, we as foreign researchers needed to understand the nuances of the native Kinyarwanda used for the student and teacher questionnaires. Our Rwandan partners had expected these questionnaires to be done in English or French. Yet had we done so, students and teachers wouldn't have been able to correctly understand the questionnaires, thus we would have risked being less accurate from a scientific standard. Therefore, we had the questionnaires carefully translated into Kinyarwanda. The questionnaires were translated into Kinyarwanda by one translator and retranslated from Kinyarwanda by a second translator. All cases of doubt were discussed with the teacher training team during a one-week workshop held before the surveys were performed. We strived to make the questionnaires as linguistically valid as possible; nevertheless due to the differences in language structure the questionnaires cannot be compared on a line-by-line basis and cannot be used in a comparative study. For example, in Kinyarwanda you cannot simply say, "I like going to school" because the action/verb requires clarification about whether you're going alone or with others. As Kinyarwanda has no words for self-responsibility or autonomy, these had to be paraphrased. Because of the many subtle linguistic issues, the bi-national team had to minutely analyze the questionnaires' content and structure, which led to a noticeable process of appropriation and finally to the ownership of the study by the Rwandan partners.

Another background for our cooperation was the fact that all parties invested a significant amount of *time* in the joint effort. The study itself lasted for only one year; however the planning and preparation phases in Rwanda and Germany took another year. The teacher training team took part in planning, carrying out and analyzing the impact evaluation in several one-week workshops. We designed the structure of this book together with the team in Rwanda who later joined us in discussing and editing text. The personal stories in the text boxes that appear throughout this book were amassed by the teacher training team in Rwanda. To acknowledge their investment of time and effort, each member of the teacher training team received a certificate from our German university describing their own individual contribution. We hope this certificate will serve our Rwandan partners as reference for future studies, e.g. in national student assessments.

Investing so much time in the project also contributed to the spirit of cooperation, as evidenced by the continuity of staff working on the project. People had a chance to know one another and build trusting relationships. While staff changes occurred within our respective teams, the key players remained throughout the duration of this study.

An appreciation of the *Rwandan culture* and the country as such also contributed to building trust and cooperation. One of the authors had formed a connection to Rwanda dating back to before the genocide. During several visits to Rwanda prior to the start of this study she'd already established many personal relationships. To her, Rwanda wasn't defined by its genocide; an attitude which was greatly appreciated by the Rwandan team. Both researchers had experience dealing with collective guilt and remembrance which also helped to establish mutual trust. Religion plays an important role in the daily lives of Rwandan teachers and teacher trainers. That the two researchers also come from religious backgrounds created another common element linking them to the Rwandans.

Curiosity probably provided the strongest impetus to creating connections. Each partner was curious about the other and really wanted to learn more. The teacher trainers discovered how their practical concrete approaches and experiences could be linked to the authors' empirical research. They derived deep satisfaction and pleasure that the results of their efforts were measurable at the student level and rose to the challenge of linking their specific experiences to the theoretical discourse. As researchers, we were incredibly enriched by discovering their colorful and lively teaching practice which continues to overcome the past and progress towards ever-better teaching methods.

As we look back at the processes of performing the research and writing this book, everyone involved kept an open mind and interacted on a deep level. We sincerely hope our readers will get a sense of the profound experiences shared and knowledge gained by all the participants in this study.

References

Abs, H., Roczen, N. & Klieme, E. (2007): Abschlussbericht zur Evaluation des BLK-Programms "Demokratie lernen und leben". [Final Report of the Evaluation of the BLK-Program "Learning and Living Democracy"] Frankfurt (Deutsches Institut für Internationale Pädagogische Forschung) (Materialien zur Bildungsforschung, Bd. 19)

Adorno, Th. W. (1966): Erziehung nach Auschwitz. [Education after Auschwitz] In: Adorno, Th. W. (1971): Erziehung zur Mündigkeit. Vorträge und Gespräche mit Hellmut Becker 1959–1969. Frankfurt/Main: Suhrkamp

Aedo-Richmond, R. & Retamal G. (ed.) (1998): Education as a humanitarian response. London/Herndorn: Cassell

AGENDA 21 (1992): Report of the United Nations Conference on Environment and Development, Rio de Janeiro, June 3–14, 1992

Akbulut-Yuksel (2009): The Long-Run Effects of Warfare and Destruction on Children: Evidence from World War II. Houston

Akresh, R. & Walque, D. de (2008): Armed Conflict and Schooling: Evidence from the 1994Rwandan Genocide. IZA Discussion Papers 3519;http://ftp.iza.org/dp3516.pdf; retrieved July 2012

Anderson, M.B. (1999): Do not harm. How aid can support peace – or war. Boulder, Colorado: Lynne Rinner Publisher

Antz, E.-M., Franz, J., Frieters, N. & Scheunpflug, A. (2009): Generationen lernen gemeinsam. Methoden für die Bildungsarbeit [Shared Intergenerationally Learning. Methods for Education] EB Spezial 11. Bielefeld: Bertelsmann

Arendt, H. (1958): The Human Condition. Chicago: Chicago University Press

Argyle, M. (1972): Soziale Interaktion. [Social Interaction] Köln: Kiepenheuer & Witsch

Arnold, N., Bekker, J., Kersh, N., Mc Leish, E. & Philips, D. (1998): Education for Reconstruction – The Regeneration of Educational Capacity Following National Upheaval. Oxford: Symposium Books

Artelt, C. & Riecke-Baulecke, Th. (2004): Bildungsstandards. Fakten, Hintergründe, Praxistipps [Standards of Education. Facts, Context, Praxis]. München: Oldenbourg

Ashcroft, K. & Raynor, P. (2011): Higher Education in Development: Lessons from Sub Saharan Africa. Information Age Publishing

Avalos, B. (2003): Improving Quality in Education – A Challenging Task? Background paper for the Education for all global monitoring report 2005: the quality imperative. Paris: UNESCO

Avalos, B. (2006): The Curriculum and Professional Development of Teachers. In: prelac journal, No. 3, December 2006. Published by the UNESCO Regional

References

Bureau of Education for Latin America and the Caribbean OREALC/UNESCO Santiago. 104–111

Bajaj, M. (ed.) (2008): Encyclopedia of Peace Education, Charlotte: Information Age

Bandura, A. (1977): Social Learning Theory. New York: General Learning Press

Bandura, A. (1997): Self-Efficacy. The Exercise of Control. New York: Freeman

Baumert, J. & Köller, O. (1998): Nationale und internationale Schulleistungsstudien. Was können sie leisten, wo sind ihre Grenzen? [National and international studies on school performance. What can they accomplish? Where are their limits?] In: Zeitschrift für Pädagogik, 50(6), 12–18

Baumert, J. & Kunter, M. (2006): Stichwort: Professionelle Kompetenz von Lehrkräften [Professional competencies of teachers]. In: Zeitschrift für Erziehungswissenschaft, [Journal for Educational Sciences] 9(4), 469–520

Bergmann, C. (2011): Abschlussbericht der Unabhängigen Beauftragten zur Aufarbeitung des sexuellen Kindesmissbrauchs. [Final Report of the Independent Commissioners on regenerating sexual child abuse] Berlin: Endformat

Bergmüller, C., Lange, S. & Scheunpflug, A. (2013): Die Verbesserung der Schuleffektivität durch In Service Trainings. Empirische Ergebnisse zweier Studien aus Kamerun. [The improvement of school efficiency by In Service Training. Empirical results of two studies from Cameroun] In: Bergmüller, Claudia (ed.): Capacity Development und Schulqualität. Konzepte und Befunde zur Lehrerprofessionalisierung in der Entwicklungszusammenarbeit, Waxmann: Münster, 127–148

Bisika, T., Ntata, P. & Konyani, S. (2009): Gender-Violence and Education in Malawi: a study of violence against girls as an obstruction to universal primary school education. In: Journal of Gender Studies, 18(3), 287–294

Bonacker, T. & Imbusch, P. (2006): Zentrale Begriffe der Friedens- und Konfliktforschung: Konflikt, Gewalt, Krieg, Frieden [Main terms of the research on peace and conflicts: conflict, violence, war, peace]. In: Imbusch, P. & Zoll, R. (eds.): Friedens- und Konfliktforschung. Eine Einführung. [research on peace and conflicts] Wiesbaden: Wochenschau, 67–142

Broutier, P. Y., Moukouri Edeme, M. & Sovoessi, J. (2005): Evaluation à mi parcours. Rapport final. Kigali

Brundtland World Commission (1987): Report of the World Commission on Environment and Development, New York: United Nations

Buckland, P. (2005): Reshaping the Future: education and postconflict reconstruction. Washington D. C.: World Bank

Bush, K.D. & Saltarelli, D. (eds.) (2000): The two faces of education in ethnic conflict. Toward a peacebuilding education for children. Florence: UNICEF

Cécé, B., Djoman, J. A. & Ranz, T. (2001): Rapport final d'évaluation du Programme de formation du personnel enseignant et administratif de l'enseignement protestant au Rwanda, Bonn

References

Center for International Education (CIE) (2006): Gender Violence in Schools: What's New? Newsletter 6. Sussex

Chen, X. & French, D.C. (2008): Children's social competence in cultural context. In: Annual Review of Psychology, 59, 591–616

Collani, G.v. & Herzberg, P.Y. (2003): Eine revidierte Fassung der deutschsprachigen Skala zum Selbstwertgefühl von Rosenberg. [The revised version of the scale on self esteem German in German by Rosenberg] Zeitschrift für Differentielle und Diagnostische Psychologie 24(1), 3–7

Conley Tyler, M.H., Bretherton, D., Halafoff, A., Nietschke, Y. (2008): Developing a peace education curriculum for Vietnamese primary schools: A case study of participatory action research in cross-cultural design. In: Journal of Research in International Education 7, 346–368

Council of Europe (ed.) (2008). Towards an active, fair and socially cohesive Europe. Report of high level task force on social cohesion. TFSC(2007)31E. Strasbourg

Csikszentmihalyi, M. (2000): Das Flow-Erlebnis. Jenseits von Angst und Langeweile im Tun aufgehen (Beyond Boredom and Anxiety – The Experience of Play in Work and Games, 1975), Stuttgart

Damasio, A. R. (1994): Descartes' Irrtum. Fühlen, Denken und das menschliche Gehirn. München

Davies, L. (2004): Education and conflict. Complexity and Chaos. New York: Routledge Falmer

Davies, L. (2010): The Potential of Human Rights Education for Conflict Prevention and Security. In: Intercultural Education, 21(5), 463–471

Davies, L., Harber, C., Schweisfurth, M., Yamashita, H. & Williams, C. (2009). Education in Emergencies in South Asia: Reducing the Risks facing Vulnerable Children. UNICEF-CIER Report

de Haan, G. (2010): The development of ESD-related competencies in supportive institutional frameworks. DOI 10.1007/s11159-010-9157-9. Published online: June 23, 2010

Delors, J. 1996. Learning: The Treasure Within. Report to UNESCO of the International Commission on Education for the Twenty-First Century, Paris: UNESCO Publishing Press

Diedrich, M., Abs, H.J. & Klieme, E. (2004): Evaluation im BLK-Modellprojekt Demokratie lernen und leben: Skalen zur Befragung von Schüler/innen, Lehrer/innen und Schulleitungen. Dokumentation der Erhebungsinstrumente 2003 [Evaluation democratical learning. Questionnaries for Students, Teachers and Principals] Franfurt/Main

Ditton, H. & Merz, D. (2000): Qualität von Schule und Unterricht. Kurzbericht über erste Ergebnisse einer Untersuchung an bayrischen Schulen. [Quality of school and lessons. Short report on first results of a research at schools in Bavaria] [www.quassu.net/Bericht1.pdf] 10.09.2010

References

Donnelly, C. (2004): What Price Harmony? Teachers' methods of delivering an ethos of peace and tolerance and respect for diversity in an integrated schools in Northern Ireland. In: Educational Research, 46(1), 3–16

Dresel, M. (2008): Dokumentation zur Erfassung der Motivation bei Grundschülern. Erlangen-Nürnberg. Universität [Documentation to record the motivation of primary school pupils]

Dresel, M. & Ziegler, A. (2006): Langfristige Förderung von Fähigkeitsselbstkonzept und Impliziter Fähigkeitstheorie durch computerbasiertes attributionales Feedback. [Long term support of ability self concepts and implicit ability theory by computer based attributional feedback] In: Zeitschrift für Pädagogische Psychologie 20, 49–63

Dunne, M. & Leach, F. (2007): Gender Conflict and Schooling: Identity, Space and Violence. In: Leach, F. & Dunne, M. (eds.). Education, Conflict and Reconciliation. International Perspectives. Bern, Switzerland: Peter Lang, 187–202

Eder, F. (2006): Schul- und Klassenklima. In: Rost, D. (ed.): Handwörterbuch Pädagogische Psychologie. Weinheim, Basel, Berlin: Beltz, 622–630 [Handbook on educational psychology]

EED = Evangelischer Entwicklungsdienst (2011): In geschwisterlicher Liebe sind wir einander zugetan. Kirchliche Partner des EED [Devoted in fraternal love. Church Partners of EED] Bonn: Brot für die Welt

EKD (2010)= Evangelische Kirche in Deutschland [3. Tagung der 11. Synode]: „Niemand darf verloren gehen!" Evangelisches Plädoyer für mehr Bildungsgerechtigkeit. [„No one should be lost". A Protestant Plea for Educational Justice]. Epd-Dokumentation 49/2010, Frankfurt/Main, Gemeinschaftswerk der Evangelischen Publizistik

Erpenbeck, J. & von Rosenstiel, L. (ed.) (2003): Handbuch Kompetenzmessung. [Handbook for the Measurement of Competencies] Stuttgart: Kohlhammer

Fleischhauer, J. (2008): Von Krieg betroffene Kinder. Eine vernachlässigte Dimension von Friedenskonsolidierung. Untersuchung psychosozialer Intervention für Kinder während und nach bewaffneten Konflikten am Beispiel Eritreas. [Children affected by war. A neglected dimension of peace consolidation. A Study of psychosocial intervention for children during and after armed conflicts on the example of Eritrea] Opladen: Budrich

Fountain, S. (1998): Education for Development: A Teacher's Resource for Global Leaning. London

Fountain, S. & UNICEF (1999): Peace Education in UNICEF. Working Paper, New York

Freedmann, S.W., Weinstein, H.M., Murphy, K. & Longman, T. (2008): Teaching History after Identity-Based Conflicts: The Rwanda Experience. In: Comparative Education Review, 52(4), 663–690

References

Fuchs, C. (2005): Selbstwirksam Lernen im schulischen Kontext. Kennzeichen – Bedingungen – Umsetzungsbeispiele. [Self-efficacy in school contexts] Ggp Media on Demand

Gaventa, J. & Barett, G. (2010): So What Difference Does it Make? Mapping out the Outcomes of Citizen Engagement. In: Institute of Development Studies (IDS) Working Paper 347

Gerecht, M., Steinert, B., Klieme, E. & Döbrich, P. (2007): Skalen zur Schulqualität: Dokumentation der Erhebungsinstrumente. Pädagogische Entwicklungsbilanzen mit Schulen (PEB). [Scales on school quality: documentation of the instruments. Educational end results of schools] Materialien zur Bildungsforschung. Band 17. Frankfurt am Main

Gillies, R. (2007): Cooperative Learning: Integrating theory and practice. London: Sage

Glasersfeld, E. (1989): Cognition, construction of knowledge, and teaching. In: Synthese, 80(1), 121–140

Gordon, T. (1981): Enseignants efficaces, Québec

Grêt, C. (2009): Le system éducatif africain en crise. Paris: Harmattan

Harber, C. (2004): Schooling as Violence. London: Routhledge Chapman & Hall

Harber, C. (2009): Toxic Schooling: How Schools Became Worse. Nottingham: Educational Heretics Press

Harries, I. & Morrison, M. L. (2003): Peace Education. North Carolina: MacFarland.

Hattie, J. A. (1992): Self-concept, Hillsdale, N.J: Psychology Press

Haußmann, W., Biener, H.-J., Hock, K. & Mokrosch, R. (eds.) (2006): Handbuch Friedenserziehung. Interreligiös – interkulturell – interkonfessionell. Gütersloher Verlagshaus: Gütersloh [Handbook on peace education. Inter-religious – intercultural – interdenominational]

Helmke, A. (1992): Selbstvertrauen und schulische Leistungen. [Self-Confidence and academic performance] Göttingen: Hogrefe

Helmke, A. (2010): Unterrichtsqualität und Lehrerprofessionalität. [Teaching Quality and Teaching Professionalism] Diagnose, Evaluation und Verbesserung des Unterrichts. 3rd edition. Seelze-Velber: Klett/Kallmeyer

Heynemann, S.P. (2000): From the Party/State to Multiethnic Democracy: Education and Social Cohesion in Europe and Central Asia. In: Educational Evaluation and Policy Analysis 22(2) (Summer 2000), 173–191

Honneth, A. (1992): The Struggle for Recognition. Moral Grammar of Social Conflicts, Boston: MIT Press

Hunt, F. (2007): Policy in Practice: Teacher-student Conflict in South African Schools. In: Leach, F. & Dunne, M. (eds.). Education, Conflict and Reconciliation. International Perspectives. Bern, Switzerland: Peter Lang, 155–168

International Network for Education in Emergencies (2013): Conflict Sensitive Education. New York.

References

Jonas, K. & Brömer, P. (2002): Die sozial-kognitive Theorie von Bandura [The social-cognitive theory of Bandura]. In: Frey, Dieter (ed.): Theorien der Sozialpsychologie: Gruppen-, Interaktions- und Lerntheorien [Theories of social psychology] (2. Aufl.). Bern, 277–299

Jungk, R. & Müllert, N. R. (1989): Zukunftswerkstätten – Mit Phantasie gegen Routine und Resignation. [Future workshops – with creativity against routine and resignation] München

Kahlert, J. (2010): Regeln ohne Werte haben keinen Wert. [Rules without values are worthless] In: Schulmanagement 5/2010, 8–10

Kammermeyer, G. & Martschinke, S. (2003): Schulleistung und Fähigkeitsselbstbild im Anfangsunterricht – Ergebnisse aus dem KILIA-Projekt. [School-Performance and Self-Perception] In: Empirische Pädagogik, 17/4, 486–503

Kanning, U.P. (2003): Diagnostik sozialer Kompetenzen. Kompendien Psychologische Diagnostik. [Diagnosis of Social Competencies. Comprisals Psychological Diagnosis] Band 4, Göttingen: Hogrefe

Klieme, E. (2004): Was sind Kompetenzen und wie lassen sie sich messen? [What are competencies and how to measure them?] In: Pädagogik 56(6), 10–13

Klieme, E., Pauli, C. & Reusser, K. (ed.). (2005): Dokumentation der Erhebungs- und Auswertungsinstrumente zur schweizerisch-deutschen Videostudie „Unterrichtsqualität, Lernverhalten und mathematisches Verständnis [Documentation of the measuring and evaluation instruments of the Swiss-German video study "Quality of lessons, learning attitudes and mathematical comprehension] part 1: Rakoczy, K., Buff, A. & Lipowsky, F. (2005). Befragungsinstrumente [Techniques of questioning](= Materialien zur Bildungsforschung, Bd. 13). Frankfurt a. M.: Deutsches Institut für internationale pädagogische Forschung (DIPF)

Klippert, H. (2009): Teamentwicklung im Klassenraum. [Team development in class room] Weinheim/Basel: Beltz.

Krogull, S. & Scheunpflug, A. (2010): Evaluation of the 'Participatory and Active Pedagogy' (PAP) run by the National Bureau of Protestant Teaching of the Protestant Council of Rwanda. Nuremberg: unpublished paper

Krupitschka, M. (1990): Selbstbild und Schulleistung, [Self image and school performance] Salzburg

Kruss, G. (2001): Towards Human Rights for South African Schools: an agenda for research and practice. In: Race, Ethnicity and Education, 4(1), 45–62

Lai, B. & Thyne, C. (2007): The Effect of Civil War on Education, 1980–97. In: Journal of Peace Research 44(3), 277–292 DOI 10.1177/0022343307076631

Lange, R. (2003): Promoting livelihood and employment in post-conflict situations. Approaches. and Lessons Learned. Stuttgart

Lange, S., Bergmüller, C., Scheunpflug, A. & Hesse, H.-G. (2010): Evaluation of the In-Service Training Programme (ISTP). Nuremberg. Unpublished paper

References

Leach, F. & Mitchell, C. (ed.) (2006): Combating Gender Violence in and around Schools. Stoke on Trent

Legendre, M.-F. (2005): La science et la technologie dans le programme de formation pour le premier cycle du secondaire: quelques clés de lecture. Spectre (Revue de l'APSQ), 35(1), 16-20.

Lenhart, V. (2010): Friedensbauende Bildungsmaßnahmen bei bewaffneten Konflikten. [Peace Building Education in Armed Conflicts] In: ZEP Zeitschrift für Internationale Bildungsforschung und Entwicklungspädagogik. [Journal for International Educational Research and Development Education] 33(4), 18-21.

Leu, E. & Price-Rom, A. (2006): Quality of Education and Teacher Learning: A Review of the Literature. U.S. Agency for International Development

Lopez, H. & Wodon, Q. (2005): The Economic Impact of Armed Conflict in Ruanda. In: Journal of African Economies, 14(4), 586-602

Lopez, H. & Wodon, Q.T. (2005): The Economic Impact of Armed Conflict in Rwanda. In: Journal of African Economies 14(4), 586-602

Luhmann, N. (1984/1995): Social Systems. Stanford: Stanford University Press

Martschinke, S. & Frank, A. (2002): Wie unterscheiden sich Schüler und Schülerinnen in Selbstkonzept und Leistung am Schulanfang? Erste Ergebnisse aus dem Kooperationsprojekt Identitäts- und Leistungsentwicklung im Anfangsunterricht KILIA. [Selfconcept and Performance of School Beginners] In: Prengel, A. & Heinzel, F. (ed.): Heterogenität, Integration und Differenzierung in der Primarstufe, 6. Band des Jahrbuches Grundschulforschung. Opladen: Leske + Budrich, 191-197

Mehreteab, A. (2002): Veteran combatants do not fade away: a comparative study on two demobilization and reintegration exercises in Eritrea; Bonn, International Center for Conversion –BICC

Merrouche, O. (2006): Economic Consequences of Wars: Evidence from Landmine Contamination in Mozambique, Economics Working Papers ECO2006/22, European University Institute, Florence

Meyer, D.L. (2009): The Poverty of Constructivism. In: Educational Philosophy and Theory. DOI: 10.1111/j.1469-5812.2008.00457.x. 41(3). 332-341

MINEDUC & InWent (2007): Pédagogie active pour renforcer la culture de la paix à l'école. Guide du facilitateur. Republique du Rwanda, Ministère de l'éducation; Centre National de Développement des Programmes (CNDP) & InWent, Capacity Building International, Germany, Kigali

MINEDUC & InWent (2008): Pédagogie active pour renforcer la culture de la paix à l'école. Manuel de l'enseignant du primaire. Republique du Rwanda, Ministère de l'éducation; Centre National de Développement des Programmes (CNDP) & InWent, Capacity Building International, Germany, Kigali

Moschner, B. & Dickhäuser, O. (2006): Selbstkonzept. [Self-Concept] In: Rost, D. H. (ed.): Handwörterbuch Pädagogische Psychologie. Weinheim: Beltz, 685-692

References

Moschner, B. (2001): Selbstkonzept [Self-Concept]. In: Rost, D. H. (ed.): Handwörterbuch Pädagogische Psychologie. Weinheim: Beltz, 629–635

Muhimpundu, F. (2002): Education et citoyenneté au Rwanda. Paris: L'Harmattan

Müller, A. (2008): Mehr ausbrüten, weniger gackern. [Hatch more, cluck less] Bern

Müller, A. & Noirjean, R. (2007): Lernerfolg ist lernbar. 22x33 handfeste Möglichkeiten, Freude am Verstehen zu kriegen. [Success in learning can be learnt. 22x33 substantial ideas to create fun when learning] Bern: Hep Verlag

Murphy, M., Stark, L., Wessells, M., Boothby, N. & Ager, A. (2011): Fortifying Barriers: sexual violence as an obstacle to girls' school participation in Northern Uganda. In: Paulson, J. (ed.). Education, Conflict and Development. Oxford: Symposium Books, 167–184

NCDC. (2005): Teaching History of Rwanda: A Participatory Approach for Secondary Schools. Kigali: National Curriculum Development Centre

Nipkow, K.E. (2007): Der schwere Weg zum Frieden. Geschichte und Theorie der Friedenspädagogik von Erasmus bis zur Gegenwart. [The difficult road to peace. History and theory of peace education from Erasmus up to the present] Gütersloh

Obura, A.P. (2003): Never Again: Educational Reconstruction in Rwanda. Paris: IIEP-UNESCO

Obura, A.P. & Bird, L. (2009): Education Marginalisation in Post-Conflict Settings: A Comparison of Government and Donor Responses in Burundi and Rwanda. Background paper prepared for the Education for All Global Monitoring Report 2010

Paccolat, J.-F. (2012): Pédagogie active et participative à la CBCA, Bukavo DRC/Fribourg, Suisse

PISA 2000 = Kunter, M., Schümer, G., Artelt, C., Baumert, J., Klieme, E., Neubrand, M., Prenzel, M., Schiefele, U., Schneider, W., Stanat, P., Tillmann, K.J. & Weiß, M. (2003): Pisa 2000 – Dokumentation der Erhebungsinstrumente. [PISA 2000 – report on the measuring instruments] Berlin: MPI für Bildungsforschung

Reißig, B. (2007): Soziale Kompetenzen. Soziale Kompetenzen sichtbar machen und für den Ausbildungs- und Berufsweg nutzen. [Social competencies. Making social competencies visible and useful for training and profession] Bericht zur Erprobung des DJI-Portfolios 'Soziale Kompetenzen'. [Report to test the DJI-portfolios 'social competencies'] München: Deutsches Jugendinstitut

Retamal, G. & Aedo-Richmond, R. (1998): Education as a Humanitarian Response. London: Cassell

Riddel, A. (2008): Factors Influencing Educational Quality and Effectiveness in Developing Countries: A Review of Research. Eschborn: Gesellschaft für Technische Zusammenarbeit (GTZ)

Rode, H. (2005): Motivation, Transfer und Gestaltungskompetenz. Ergebnisse der Abschlussevaluation des BLK-Programms "21". [Motivation, Transfer, and

References

Shaping Competence. Results of the final evaluation of the BLK-program '21'] 1999–2004 (Berlin, BLK)

Rolff, H.-G. (2007): Studien zu einer Theorie der Schulentwicklung. Weinheim, Basel: Beltz Verlag [Studies on a theory of school development]

Rose-Krasnor, L. (1997): The Nature of Social Competence: A Theoretical Review. In: Social Development 6, DOI 10.1111/j.1467-9507.1997.tb00097.x, 111–135.

Rost, D., Schermer, F. (2006): Leistungsängstlichkeit. [Fear of performance] In: Rost, D.H. (ed.): Handwörterbuch Pädagogische Psychologie. Weinheim: Beltz, 404–416

Roth, G. (2001): Fühlen, Denken, Handeln. Wie das Gehirn unser Verhalten steuert. [Feeling, thinking, acting. How the brain steers our behaviour] Frankfurt/M.

Runde, B. (2001): Instrumente zur Messung sozialer Kompetenzen. [Instrument of measuring social competences] In: Zeitschrift für Psychologie, 210(4), 186–196

Rutayisire, J. (2007): The Role of Teachers in the Social and Political Reconstruction of Post-genocide Rwanda. In: Leach, F. & Dunne, M. (eds.). Education, Conflict and Reconciliation. International Perspectives. Bern, Switzerland: Peter Lang, 115–130

Rutayisire, J., Kabano, J. & Rubagisa, J. (2004): Redefining Rwanda's future: The Role of Curriculum in Social Reconstruction. In: Tawil, S. & Harley, A. (eds.). Education, Conflict and Social Cohesion. Geneva: UNESCO, International Bureau of Education, 315–373

Rychen, D.S. & Salganik, L.H. (eds.) (2001): Defining and Selecting Key Competencies. Göttingen: Hogrefe and Huber Publications

Rychen, D.S. & Salganik, L.H. (eds.) (2003): Key Competencies for a Successful Life and a Well-Functioning Society. Göttingen

Salmi, J. (2006): Violence, Democracy and Education: an Analytic Framework. In: Roberts-Schweitzer, E., Greaney, V. & Duer, K. (eds.). Promoting Social Cohesion through Education. Washington D.C.

Sarason, B.R. (1981): The dimensions of social competence. Contributions from a variety of research areas. In: Wine, J.D. & Smye, M.D. (eds.): Social competence. New York: Guilford Press

Scheerens, J. & Bosker, J. (1997): The foundations of educational effectiveness. Oxford

Schell-Faucon, S. (2001/2002): Developing education and youth-promotion measures in with focus on peace building and conflict prevention. Eschborn: GTZ

Schell-Faucon, S. (2001a): Bildungs- und Jugendförderung mit friedenspädagogischer und konfliktpräventiver Zielrichtung. [Promotion of education and youth aiming at peace education and conflict prevention] Eschborn: GTZ

Schell-Faucon, S. (2001b). Journey into the inner self and encounter with the other. Johannesburg: CSVR. Verfügbar unter: http://www.csvr.org.za/papers/papschel.html (download 7. 3. 2003).

References

Scherg, N. & GTZ (2003): Entwicklungsorientierte Traumabearbeitung in Nachkriegssituationen. [Development-Oriented Treatment of Trauma in Post-War Situations] Eschborn. Download on January 5 2010

Scheunpflug, A. (2001): Biologische Grundlagen des Lernens, [Biological foundations of learning] Cornelsen: Scriptor

Scheunpflug, A. (2006): Gefühle als Helfer. Körpereigene Bewertungssysteme [Feelings as assistants. Endogenic assessment systems]. In: Lernen. Wie sich Kinder und Jugendliche Wissen und Fähigkeiten aneignen. [Learning. How children and young people adopt knowledge and abilities] Seelze: Friedrich-Verlag, 34–36.

Scheunpflug, A., Bergmüller, C. & Moukouri, M. (2011): Der Beitrag von Schulentwicklung zur Chancengerechtigkeit – eine Fallanalyse aus dem evangelischen Privatschulwesen in Kamerun. [The Contribution of School Development to Social Justice – a Case Study from Protestant Schools in Cameroon] In: Zeitschrift für Internationale Bildungsforschung und Entwicklungspädagogik ZEP 34(1), 38–41

Scheunpflug, A. & Schröck, N. (2003) Globales Lernen. [Global Learning] Stuttgart

Scheunpflug A., Stadler-Altmann, U. & Zeinz H. (2012): Bestärken und Fördern. Wege zu einer veränderten Lernkultur in der Sekundarstufe I [Encouraging and Supporting. Path ways to a Changing Learning Culture in Lower Secondary Schools]. Seelze: Kallmeyer-Klett 2012

Schoon, I. (2009): Measuring social competencies. Working paper no 58. Council for Social and Economic Data (RatSWD), Berlin http://ssrn.com/abstract=1447882

Schröder, A., Rademacher, H. & Merkle, A. (ed.) (2008): Handbuch Konflikt- und Gewaltpädagogik, Schwalbach: Wochenschau [Handbook conflict and violence education]

Schwarzer, R. & Jerusalem, M. (1999): Skalen zur Erfassung von Lehrer- und Schülermerkmalen: Dokumentation der psychometrischen Verfahren im Rahmen der wissenschaftlichen Begleitung zum Modellversuch Selbstwirksame Schule. Berlin

Seitz, K. (2004): Education and Conflict. The Role of Education in the creation, prevention and resolution of social crises. Consequences for development cooperation. Eschborn: Gesellschaft für Technische Zusammenarbeit (GTZ)

Seitz, K. (2006): Das Janusgesicht der Bildung. Schlüssel für eine zukunftsfähige Entwicklung oder Entwicklungshemmnis? [The Janus Face of Education: Key to a sustainable education or a barrier for development?] In: Zeitschrift für internationale Bildungsforschung und Entwicklungspädagogik [Journal for international educational research and development education] 29(1/2), 33–39

Shavelson, R. J., Hubner, J. J. & Stanton, G. C. (1976): Self-Concept: Validation of Construct Interpretations. Review of Educational Research 46, 407–441

Shemyakina, O. (2006): The Effect of Armed Conflict on Accumulation of Schooling: Results from Tajikistan, HiCN Working Papers 12

References

Silbereisen, R.K. (1995): Soziale Kognition: Entwicklung von sozialem Wissen und Verstehen [Social cognition: development of social kowledge and understanding] in: Oerter, R. & Montada, L. (eds.). Entwicklungspsychologie [development psychology], Weinheim: Psychologie Verlags Union, 823–861

Singh, M. (2003): Understanding Life Skills, Background Paper for the Education for All. Global Monitoring Report 2003/4, Gender and Education for All: The Leap to Equality. Downloaded on 30 October 2010 at http://unesdoc.unesco.org/images/0014/001469/146963e.pdf

Smith, A. & Vaux, T. (2003): Education, conflict and international development. London: DFID

Sommers, M. (1999): Emergency Education for Children. Cambridge, MA: Mellon Foundation/MIT

Stadler-Altmann, U. (2010): Das Schülerselbstkonzept. Eine empirische Annäherung, [Self Concept of Students. An Empircial Approach] Bad Heilbrunn: Klinkhardt

Stanat, P. & Kunter, M. (2001): Kooperation und Kommunikation [Cooperation and Communication] In: Deutsches PISA-Konsortium (ed.). PISA 2000. Opladen: Leske & Budrich, 300–321

Stanat, P., Scheunpflug, A., Kuper, H., Thiel, F. & Hannover, B. (2010): Assessment as a Tool for Evidence-Based Development of Post-Elementary Educational Opportunities in Developing Countries. Berlin: Unpublished Paper

Standfest, C., Köller, O. & Scheunpflug, A (2005): Leben – Lernen – Glauben. Zur Qualität evangelischer Schulen. Eine empirische Untersuchung über die Leistungsfähigkeit von Schulen in evangelischer Trägerschaft. [Life – learning – believe. On quality of protestant schools. An empirical research on the performance of Protestant schools] Waxmann: Münster/Berlin

Storeng, M. (2001): Giving Learners a Chance. Learner-Centredness in the Reform of Namibian Teaching. Studies in Comparative and International Education, Vol. 56, Stockholm: Stockholm University Press

Tatto, M.T. (2007): Reforming Teaching Globally. Oxford Studies in Comparative Education. Oxford: Symposium Books

Tawil, S. & Harley, A. (eds.) (2004): Education, conflict, and social cohesion. Studies in Comparative Education. Geneva: IBE UNESCO

Taylor, P. (1998): Constructivism: Value added. In: Fraser, B. & Tobin, K. (eds.). The International handbook of science education. Dordrecht, The Netherlands: Kluwer Academic, 1111–1123

Tschannen-Moran, M., Woolfolk Hoy, A.W. & Hoy, W.K. (1998): Teachers efficacy: Its meaning and measure. In: Review of Educational Research, 68(2), 202–248

UNESCO (2000): 'Manifesto 2000'. Available at: http://www3.unesco.org/manifesto2000/default.asp

References

UNESCO (2010): The qualitative impact of conflict on education. Think peace commissioned for the EfA Global Monitoring Report 2011. The hidden crisis: Armed conflict and education. Montreal: UNESCO Institute of Statistics

UNESCO (2010): The qualitative impact of conflict on education. Think peace commissioned for the EfA Global Monitoring Report 2011, The hidden crisis: Armed conflict and education. Montreal: UNESCO Institute of Statistics

UNESCO (2011 a): Methodological Guide for the Analysis of Teacher Issues. Teacher Training Initiative for Sub-Saharan Africa (TTISSA), Teacher Policy Development Guide, Dakar

UNESCO (2011): The hidden crisis: Armed conflict and education. EFA Global Monitoring Report 2011, Paris: UNESCO

v. Hentig, H. (1985): Die Menschen stärken, die Sachen klären. Ein Plädoyer für die Wiederherstellung der Aufklärung. [Reinforcing Persons, Clarify Things. A Plea for Enlightment], Stuttgart: Reclam-Verlag

Verspoor, A.M. (2008): The challenge of learning. Improving the quality of basic education in Sub-Saharan Africa. In: Johnson, D. (ed.). The changing landscape of education in Africa. Quality, equality and democracy. Oxford: Symposium Books, 13–43

Wang, M.C., Haertel, G.D. & Walberg, H.J. (1993): Toward a knowledge base for school learning. In: Review of Educational Research (Washington, DC), 63, 249–294

Weinbrenner, P. & Häcker, W. (1991): Zur Theorie und Praxis von Zukunftswerkstätten [Theory and practice of future workshops]. In: Bundeszentrale für politische Bildung (ed.): Methoden in der politischen Bildung – Handlungsorientierung. Methods in political education – acting orientated] Band 304. Bonn, 115–149

Weinert, F.E. (2001): Concept of Competence: A Conceptual Classification. In: Rychen, D.S. & Salganik, L.H. (ed.): Defining and selecting key competencies. Seattle, 45–65

Welsh, J. & Biermann, K.L. (2001): Social Competence. In: Encyclopedia of Childhood and Adolescence. Downloaded on 20 April 2011 at

White, C.S. (1998): From the Party/State to Multi-Ethnic Democracy: Education and Its Influence on Social Cohesion in the Europe and Central Asia Region. Alexandria, Virginia: ERIC ED 428015

Winkel, Rainer (1996): Der gestörte Unterricht, Cornelsen: Berlin [The disturbed lesson]

Winter-Ebmer, R. (1998): Potential Unemployment Benefit Duration and Spell Length: Lessons from a Quasi-Experiment in Austria, In: Oxford Bulletin of Economics and Statistics, 33–46

Yu, G. (2007): Research evidence of school effectiveness in Sub-Sahara African Countries. EDQUAL Working Paper. Effectiveness No. 2, Bristol, UK, University of Bristol

References

Zeinz, H. (2006): Schulische Selbstkonzepte und soziale Vergleiche in der Grundschule: Welche Rolle spielt die Einführung von Schulnoten? [Self-Concept and Social Comparison in Primary Education – Which Roles Play Marks?] Dissertation. Universitätsbibliothek Erlangen-Nürnberg

Ziegler, A., Dresel, M., Schober, B. & Stöger, H. (2005): Motivationstestbatterie für Schülerinnen und Schüler der Jahrgangsstufen 5–10 (MTB 5–10): Skalendokumentation. [Sets to test out the motivation of students in school year 5 to 10]Ulm: Universität

About the Authors

Susanne Krogull is a researcher at Otto-Friedrich-University Bamberg/Germany where she serves as Executive Director of the international Master's program, "Educational Quality in Developing Countries". Her research interest is focused on educational quality, international and comparative education and Global Education. She has broad practical experiences in Global Learning acquired in different NGOs.

Prof. Dr. Annette Scheunpflug holds the chair of Foundations in Education/Philosophy of Education at Otto-Friedrich-University Bamberg/ Germany. As a former primary teacher, she has broad experiences in teaching and teacher education. Her research interest is focused on educational quality, international and comparative education, Global Education, and anthropology of education.

François Rwambonera served as the head of the National Bureau of Protestant Education in Kigali/Rwanda until 2013. As a former secondary teacher, he has a broad experience in teaching and teacher education. After the genocide in Rwanda, he – and his team – developed the adopted approach of learner-centered education – called "Participative and Active Pedagogy" – as an educational response to the post-conflict situation in his country.

With contributions from
Pierre Claver Bisanze, Innocent Gasana, Rudolf Heinrichs-Drinhaus, Immaculée Mukantabana, Violette Mukayisenga, Anastasie Mukaruberwa, Marlène Mukandoli, Anathalie Munganyinka Félicité Musabyemariya, Samuel Mutabazi, Théophile Mutuyeyezu, Jean-Baptiste Ndamukunda, Jean Bosco Ndimubanzi, Jean Baptiste Ndigendereho, Silas Nsengiyumva, Agnès Nyirangirimana, Capitolina Nyirabazamanza, Josée Nyiramana, Monique Nyirandikumana, Athalie Nyiranzigiyimana, Christian Grêt, Athanase Rutayisire, Gérard Ugirashebuja, Césarie Uwabaganwa, and Zacharie Zikama

Neda Forghani-Arani, Helmuth Hartmeyer,
Eddi O'Loughlin, Liam Wegimont (Eds.)

Global Education in Europe

Policy, Practice and
Theoretical Challenges

Erziehungswissenschaft und Weltgesellschaft, Vol. 6
2013, 216 pages, pb, € 24,90
ISBN 978-3-8309-2897-3
E-Book: 21,90 €, ISBN 978-3-8309-7897-8

With this book, GENE – Global Education Network Europe – marks ten years of work. It explores key contemporary issues in Global Education and outlines challenges in research, practice, policy and conceptual development. The book will be of use to policymakers, educationalists, researchers, and practitioners in the fields of education, international development, human rights and sustainability.

Christel Adick (Hrsg.)

Bildungsentwicklungen und Schulsysteme in Afrika, Asien, Lateinamerika und der Karibik

Historisch-vergleichende Sozialisations- und Bildungsforschung, Band 11
2013, 320 Seiten, br., 34,90 €
ISBN 978-3-8309-2785-3
E-Book-Preis: 30,99 €

Bildungsentwicklungen außerhalb der ‚westlichen' Welt sind Thema dieses Sammelbandes. Teil 1 enthält Regionalstudien zu Bildung in den Arabischen Staaten, der Karibik, Lateinamerika, den Ostasiatischen Staaten, der Pazifikregion, Subsahara-Afrika und Süd- und Westasien. In Teil 2 finden sich Länderstudien zum Bildungswesen einzelner Staaten dieser Regionen: Brasilien, China, Nigeria, Indien, Japan, Mexiko und Südafrika.

Trotz der Vielfältigkeit und -schichtigkeit des Themas gelingt der bezweckte ‚Rundumschlag' durch die Mischung aus grundlegendem Überblickswissen und regional übergreifenden Aussagen. Damit stellt die Publikation eine ausgezeichnete Grundlagenlektüre dar, um sich in die relevanten historischen und aktuellen Entwicklungen der Schul- und Bildungswesen von Ländern der Entwicklungszusammenarbeit einzuarbeiten.

Sarah Lange in: ZEP 3/2013

Sabine Hornberg, Claudia Richter, Carolin Rotter (Hrsg.)

Erziehung und Bildung in der Weltgesellschaft

2013, 286 Seiten, br., 39,90 €
ISBN 978-3-8309-2921-5
E-Book-Preis: 35,99 €

In Christel Adicks Arbeiten zur International und Interkulturell vergleichenden Erziehungswissenschaft wird ersichtlich, dass Fragen der Bildung und Erziehung nicht länger nur auf der Folie nationalstaatlicher Entwicklungen erörtert und bearbeitet werden dürfen, sondern weltgesellschaftlichen Entwicklungen Rechnung tragen müssen. Die Beiträge dieses Bandes, an dem Weggefährtinnen und Weggefährten sowie akademische Schülerinnen und Schüler von Christel Adick mitgewirkt haben, reflektieren das Anliegen, die Ideen und Schriften von Christel Adick und die Resonanz, die ihre Arbeit auch über die International und Interkulturell Vergleichende Erziehungswissenschaft hinaus findet, zu würdigen.

www.ingramcontent.com/pod-product-compliance
Lightning Source LLC
Chambersburg PA
CBHW051814230426
43672CB00012B/2729